Celebrations for young people

Celebrations for young people

Fully worked-out Services with readings,
prayers, activity ideas & music

KATIE THOMPSON

Kevin
Mayhew

First published in 2001 by
KEVIN MAYHEW LTD
Buxhall, Stowmarket
Suffolk IP14 3BW

9 8 7 6 5 4 3 2 1 0

ISBN 1 84003 723 7
Catalogue No 1500419

Cover illustration by Jonathan Stroulger
Edited by Katherine Laidler
Typesetting by Louise Selfe
Printed in Great Britain

Contents

Introduction

Where two or three are gathered together in my name,
I am there with them.
Matthew 18:20

Celebration is at the heart of Christian life. It allows us to open ourselves to God's many gifts through prayer, praise, thanksgiving and forgiveness. As we joyfully express our sense of community and belonging, together we learn to recognise and appreciate God's loving action in our everyday lives.

When given a suitable opportunity, young people are just as capable as adults of encountering God and developing a meaningful personal relationship with him. This book introduces children to a variety of celebration experiences, intended to lead them to a deeper understanding of and participation in the liturgy, through meditative prayer and relaxation, appropriate Scripture texts, activities, music, signs and symbols, and a deepening awareness of their individual spirituality through guided visualisations and prayerful silence.

The themes have been chosen to reflect and celebrate the love, hopes, fears and concerns which are at the heart of young people's lives. They can be used in many different ways in the classroom, at assemblies, school Masses, retreat weekends or days of reflection, prayer services, in confirmation or youth groups, and within the context of parish worship and celebrations with young people. Each theme is reflected in readings, prayers, activity ideas and music, which, with careful planning and co-operation, can be integrated with what is being taught in other subjects within the school environment.

This resource material is flexible to allow you to use it with imagination and freedom with a broad spectrum of age groups, ranging from primary school to teenagers. The practical ideas and suggestions for reflections and prayers should be adapted appropriately for the individual needs and capabilities of the group or for a particular situation. The effectiveness of symbolism, and how much younger children can gain from it, should not be underestimated. Similarly, a simple liturgy or practical activity, which is thoughtfully presented and used in the appropriate environment, can deliver a powerful message to older age groups. Use the material as a spring-board which inspires your imagination and encourages you to develop your own creative ideas. Any tool is only as good as the person using it, and to breathe life, excitement, joy and enthusiasm into this resource, you need first to make the material your own.

These celebrations enable young people to gather together and bring before the Lord a simple liturgy in which they share, and can relate to and understand. In a setting of love, openness and security, they have the opportunity to open themselves to the action of God's Holy Spirit as they celebrate the joy and challenge of the Good News and what it means in their young lives.

Katie Thompson

Practical suggestions

With care it is possible to create a worshipful atmosphere almost anywhere.

- It is important to have a focal point arranged simply and prayerfully well in advance, to help create an atmosphere conducive to celebration and prayer. With a little careful forethought this provides a powerful and effective visual aid for specific themes. It also serves to capture the children's attention and to visually reinforce a message or point of reflection. When working with young people it is important to recognise the value of referring to what is most relevant and important to them – news and current affairs, sport, pop music – bearing in mind the principle that life and faith are inseparably connected.

- Arrange the space in which you gather carefully, paying particular attention to seating and any movement the group might be required to make during a celebration. Check that the room is comfortably warm, and, if possible and practical, soften the lighting to improve the general ambience. If fluorescent lights are the only option, then candles can be used to great effect (with obvious care and regard for safety). Subtle fragrance from a candle or incense burner can add to the atmosphere, but take care that such fragrances are not too strong or likely to cause anyone discomfort.

- The passages of Scripture provided have been drawn from both the Old and New Testament and chosen to reflect each theme. For any reading from Scripture it is good to have a Bible displayed in a prominent position with its importance highlighted, perhaps by a candle or simple flower arrangement. The texts provided for each celebration have been adapted for young people to read and understand. If they are to be read by a child, a printed sheet can be placed on or in the Bible. This reminds everyone that they are listening to God's Word as he speaks to us through the Holy Scriptures. A brief reflection follows the reading. This is intended as a guide and to give suggestions and ideas for a homily or discussion.

- Children and young people often prefer the floor when it comes to meditation! Therefore this should be clean and preferably carpeted. If this proves difficult, then simply use chairs. Sitting comfortably, or leaning forward on to a desk, with arms and head resting on a rolled-up jumper or soft bag, provides a perfectly acceptable alternative.

- Suitable background music can be very valuable to help set a scene or mood, and to draw attention away from background noise. 'Seamless' tapes or CDs of natural sounds, such as the sea or a flowing river, are a useful option which help particularly with relaxation when played quietly in the background. Remember that for some this may be a completely new and unfamiliar experience, and they may need time to learn how to enter into the stillness of contemplative prayer and silence.

- A selection of music and hymns is suggested for each celebration. The letters in brackets refer to *Liturgical Hymns Old and New* (LitHON) (Kevin Mayhew, 1999) or *Our Songs* (OS) (Kevin Mayhew, 1998).

1

We celebrate God's coming

Focus   A 'manger' filled with hay to represent Christ of the past; a chalice/cup and a bunch of grapes and some bread to represent Christ of the present; a Bible opened at Matthew 25:31-46 and a clock to represent Christ of the future. (Have the room darkened or softly lit as people arrive.)

Introduction   During the season of Advent we think about the coming of Christ:

> Christ of the past,
> who was laid in a manger.

> Christ of the present,
> who feeds us with his body and blood.

> Christ of the future,
> who will come again in glory.

Sing 'Away in a manger'.

Penitential reflection   Son of God made man:
Lord, forgive us.
Lord, forgive us.

Friend of the friendless, and Saviour of all:
Christ, forgive us.
Christ, forgive us.

Light of the world and Prince of peace:
Lord, forgive us.
Lord, forgive us.

(Carefully and slowly, light a candle on either side of the place where God's Word is to be proclaimed.)

Scripture   *Old Testament reading – adapted from Isaiah 9:1-7*

The people that walked in darkness
have seen a great light.
On those who lived in a land of deep shadow
a light has shone.
You have increased their happiness,
you have made their joy greater.
For a child is born for us,
a Son given to us, and he will rule over us.
He will be called 'Wonder-Counsellor',
'Mighty-God', 'Eternal-Father',
and 'Prince-of-Peace'.
He will reign in everlasting peace,
from this time onwards and for ever.

Gospel – adapted from Luke 2:1-14

Caesar Augustus, the Roman Emperor, ordered a census to be taken, and everyone returned to the town of their family origin to be registered. So it was that Joseph and Mary left Nazareth in Galilee and returned to Bethlehem in Judaea, King David's childhood home. All this came to pass because Joseph was a descendant of David's royal line. While they were there, the time came for Mary to have her baby, and she wrapped him in strips of cloth and laid him in a manger, because there was no room at the inn.

On a hillside near the town, some shepherds were watching over their sheep. Suddenly, an angel appeared and the sky was filled with God's glory. The shepherds were terrified, but the angel said, 'Do not be afraid, for I have great news for you. Today a baby has been born in Bethlehem; he is Christ the Lord. You will find him lying in a manger.' The sky was filled with the sound of angels singing, 'Glory to God in the highest, and peace to all people on earth!'

Reflection   *An alternative account of the Christmas story – according to the angels!*

God called a meeting of his angels and archangels. 'I have decided that my Son Jesus will be born tonight as a human child in a stable in Bethlehem,' he announced as he pointed to a carefully marked 'X' on a map of Judaea. 'Did he say, "stable"?' asked one of the angels, 'Yes, but I'm sure he meant to say, "palace",' added another. 'Make sure that there is plenty of hay for the manger, and clean strips of cloth handy for Mary his mother to wrap him in,' God continued.

The angels ruffled their feathers in disbelief and were deeply concerned. 'There must be some mistake!' they exclaimed. 'Surely God doesn't mean this very night! There is far too much to arrange beforehand. The angelic choirs will need more time for rehearsals, and there is so much to organise and plan before the whole world can celebrate such a unique and joyful event properly. And as for the idea of setting all this in a smelly old stable!' And great debates about God's low-key plans broke out among the ranks of angels.

To put an end to all this squabbling, the angel Gabriel, who was one of God's favourite messengers, decided to check out God's plan and get some answers from the Boss himself. God smiled and listened patiently as Gabriel carefully explained the angels' concerns that perhaps a palace would be more appropriate for the birth of his beloved Son than a stable with hay and strips of swaddling; and how they would need more time to arrange suitably important visitors to welcome this very special child into the world, because an ox and ass were all that were available at such short notice; and then there was the problem of . . .

But God stopped Gabriel before he could go any further. 'My Son will be born in humility to serve the world in humility,' he said. 'Do not worry, Gabriel, his glory and power will be revealed all in good time and according to my carefully prepared plan.'

Now Gabriel knew that although he seldom understood God's plans for the world and the people he loved above all else, they always seemed to work out just fine. After all, he had made rather a good job of creation! So after further discussion with God, Gabriel returned to the hosts of angels and explained everything the Almighty had told him.

Later that same night, everything came to be, just as God had planned. Christ the Saviour of the world was born in the humble surroundings of a simple stable, and wrapped in swaddling cloths by Mary his loving mother.

God was so touched by the concern of Gabriel and the other angels that he was persuaded to make one final adjustment to his perfect plan. And so it came about that Gabriel and his fellow angels were allowed to announce their news of great joy to an unsuspecting group of shepherds on a hillside – the only available audience at that time of night – and, despite a serious lack of rehearsal time, wow them with their enthusiastic heavenly tunes as together they sang, 'Glory to God in the highest heaven, and peace to all people on earth'.

More than two thousand years have gone by since the Son of God was born in a place called Bethlehem, and laid lovingly in a manger by Mary his mother. Every year, during the season of Advent, we remember and retell the events which led up to the birth of our Saviour, Jesus Christ. We recall that God's love for the world was, and still is, so great that he sent his only beloved Son to show us the way to his love and his kingdom.

And yet, as we are caught up in the busy preparations for the Christmas celebrations, we need to remind ourselves that Jesus isn't simply someone who belongs in the past events of two thousand years ago, or someone who has promised to return at some unknown time in the future. He is here now – God living with us in the present. We bump into him every day in the people we meet all around us. So perhaps as Christmas draws closer, we should ask ourselves, 'Do we welcome Jesus into our lives every day, or do we restrict our welcome to this special time once a year?'

Intercession   As we recall Christ's first coming
and prepare for his return,
let us turn to God our loving Father
who sent his only Son to be our Saviour,
as we pray:

For all who hunger;
that we will feed their hunger for food and love
in our world today.

Silence

Lord, hear our prayer:
may we make you welcome.

For all who thirst;
that we will quench their thirst
for justice and equal rights
in our world today.

Silence

Lord, hear our prayer:
may we make you welcome.

For all who are alone;
that we will welcome them
and make them feel that they belong
in our world today.

Silence

Lord, hear our prayer:
may we make you welcome.

For all who are poor and naked;
that we clothe them with our love
and show them that we care.

Silence

Lord, hear our prayer:
may we make you welcome.

Father,
in the hustle and bustle
of Christmas excitement and preparations,

may we make time to welcome you
in the ordinariness of the everyday people
whom we meet in our everyday lives,
so that we will be ready to greet you
when you return in glory.
We ask this through Christ our Lord.
Amen.

Activities and ideas

- *Liturgy of welcome*
  Give each child a pen and a strip of paper to represent a piece of swaddling cloth. With suitable music playing softly (for example, 'Away in a manger'), invite them to reflect about, and then write down, a way in which they can make Jesus welcome in their everyday lives. Their pieces of swaddling can be brought up one at a time, and arranged on the manger which is a focal part of the celebration.

- On a table, which is placed at a suitably safe distance from the central focus, place a large candle to represent Christ the Light of the World, surrounded by nightlights and copies of the poem below, sufficient to provide one for each child. During the Old Testament reading, light the large candle in the centre. Then invite each child to come forward and, using a taper, light their nightlight from the central candle before collecting a copy of 'A Christmas reflection' to keep. Gentle music should be playing in the background (for example, 'Christ be our Light') as the room gradually grows brighter and is filled with light.

  A Christmas reflection
  Could it be true?
  This most amazing tale of all . . .
  the maker of the stars and sea
  became a child on earth for me?

  That in the stillness of the night,
  beneath a star's shining light,
  a woman smiled as she gave birth,
  and Christ was born to save God's earth.

16

Yes it is true!
Some shepherds were the first to hear
the angels' heralds of good cheer.
A Saviour born that very night,
transforming darkness into light.

- Perform a simple dramatisation of the angels' version of the Christmas story.

Music

- Away in a manger (LitHON/OS)
- Longing for light (Christ be our light) (LitHON)
- Come, come, come to the manger (LitHON/OS)
- While shepherds watched (LitHON/OS)
- Come, Lord Jesus, come (LitHON/OS)

2

Lenten journey

Focus   A large crucifix or simple cross made from two wooden cross-pieces bound together and placed on a background piece of purple fabric; a Bible opened at Matthew 16:24; a large candle; a tray filled with damp sand and the impression of two footprints.

Introduction   The season of Lent begins on Ash Wednesday when ashes are traditionally blessed and used as a sign of repentance and a reminder of the dust from which we are created and to which we will one day return. It should not be a time of doom and gloom, which we only associate with hardship and misery as we try to think of ways to give up some of our pleasures in life. It should be a season of renewal, of new beginnings and fresh opportunities for drawing closer to God. It should be a special time when we open ourselves up to God's grace, and walk closely beside him as we make our Lenten journey towards Easter and the joyful celebration of Christ's resurrection.

Penitential reflection   Peter asked Jesus this question, 'Lord, if someone sins against me again and again, how many times should I forgive that person? As many as seven times?' In reply Jesus said, 'Not just seven times, Peter, but seventy-seven times.' (Matthew 18:21-22)

For the times
when we harden our hearts
and are unforgiving towards one another:
Lord, have mercy.
Lord, have mercy.

For the times
when we are quick to point out the faults of others,
without recognising our own:
Christ, have mercy.
Christ, have mercy.

For the times
when we allow selfish words and actions
to lead us away from God's love and friendship:
Lord, have mercy.
Lord, have mercy.

Scripture   *Old Testament reading – adapted from 1 Kings 19:4-8*

Elijah had walked through the wilderness for a whole day, until finally he slumped exhausted beneath the shade of a small bush and tried to escape from the heat of the fearsome sun. He was totally fed-up. 'Lord, take my life,' he pleaded. 'I would rather die now than take another wretched step,' he muttered, before falling into a deep sleep.

Some time later he was wakened by an angel sent from God. 'Elijah get up and have something to eat and drink,' the angel said, and Elijah discovered a freshly baked scone and a jar of water had appeared beside him. So he ate and drank before falling asleep once again. Then the angel returned for a second time, and again encouraged Elijah to have something to eat and drink. 'Unless you eat and drink you will not have enough strength for your journey,' the angel told him. So Elijah did as the angel had said, and feeling refreshed and strengthened, he set off to complete his long journey to Mount Horeb.

New Testament reading – adapted from Ephesians 4:25-26, 32-5:20

From now on, be honest and tell no lies to one another, because, after all, we each belong to the one body of Christ. If someone makes you angry, sort out your argument with them before the end of the day when the sun sets, so that the anger you feel is not carried in your heart to spoil another day. Be kind and understanding towards one another, and ready to forgive as willingly as God forgives you. Above all, as God's children, follow his example of goodness and try to love one another as much as he loves you.

Gospel – adapted from Matthew 26:37-39 and Luke 22:41-44

When they had finished eating supper together, Jesus and his disciples made their way to the Garden of Gethsemane, where Jesus was overwhelmed by fear and dread. His heart was almost crushed by the sadness he felt, and he was seized by a terrible fear of the suffering which lay ahead of him. In his despair he cried aloud, 'Father, if it is possible, take this cup of suffering away from me!' But then he added, 'Let everything happen according to your will and not mine.' As he continued to pray, his sweat fell to the ground like droplets of blood, and an angel from God appeared to comfort and strengthen him for what lay ahead.

Reflection

Jesus and Elijah had a great deal in common. Both were filled with despair at the thought of the journeys God wanted them to make. Sometimes, as we begin our Lenten journey, the thought of six weeks of special effort and self-denial can fill us with a certain amount of despair and reluctance too! Neither of them wanted to take the next step along the road they were expected to follow, and in their desperation they both turned to God for consolation. God heard their cries for help and responded with the support and strength which they needed at that particular moment. For Elijah that meant feeding him so that he would be sufficiently revived and refreshed to carry on his way. God feeds and nourishes us too, not just as we make our journey through Lent, but as we each make our own personal journey through life. Jesus said, 'I am the living bread which has come down from heaven.' By feeding us at the table of his Word and the table of the Eucharist, he helps us to know and love him more in our everyday lives.

So ask yourself: this Lent will I make a special effort to spend time reading or listening to God's Word? Will I try to meet the person of Jesus more often through the sacraments of Reconciliation and Holy Communion?

In the agony in the garden, we perhaps see Jesus at his most human and vulnerable. The Son of God made man, whose only 'crime' was to love and be loved, knew what suffering awaited him on his journey to the cross on Calvary, and he was afraid. We all know how it feels to anticipate something which we dread. It might be something we must do in public, perhaps an exam or an operation, or it may be something as simple as a visit to the dentist! Although our fear cannot compare with Christ's agony in the garden, we too will often find ourselves calling on God in prayer to help us get through our moment of difficulty.

So ask yourself: this Lent will I make an extra effort to spend more time getting to know God through prayer? Will I be prepared to try out new ways of praying?

Sometimes we need to remind ourselves that although God always hears our prayers and responds to help us, that response is often apparent not so much in the extraordinary but in the ordinary events and people around us, as this little story illustrates so well!

There was once a man who loved God and had complete faith in him. When it began to rain so hard that the basement of his house filled with water, he was not unduly concerned. 'God will save me if the floods continue to rise,' he told himself as he moved his belongings upstairs. The rain continued to fall night and day, and as the water steadily rose a man in a canoe came by and offered to rescue the man from his flooded house. 'There's no need,' he replied. 'I know that God will save me.' As the water rose still further, the man in the house retreated upstairs to the next floor. Another boat came past, and again its occupants offered to rescue him from his house, which by this time was rapidly disappearing beneath the water. But again he refused, as he cheerfully declared, 'God will save me!' Finally the man was forced to take shelter on the roof of his house, but when a helicopter flew by and offered to pluck him to safety – yes, you've already guessed – the man refused their help and decided to wait for God to save him.

Eventually the flood water swept him away and the poor man drowned! When he arrived still dripping at heaven's pearly gates, he was ready to give God a piece of his mind. 'I had complete faith in you,' he told God angrily. 'I believed that you would save me and yet you let me drown!' God said to him, 'I tried to rescue you three times – first by canoe, then by boat, and when you still refused to listen, I even sent a helicopter.'

Unlike the man in the story, we must be open to recognising the fact that God often answers our prayers through the actions and words of those around us. In times of need, it is our giving and our reaction which forms God's response to the prayers of others in need. In times of difficulty and disaster, he answers their cries for help by working through us and our generous donations and efforts to ease their suffering. He depends on ordinary people working in ordinary ways to achieve the extraordinary.

So, finally, ask yourself: this Lent will I make a special effort to give generously to others? Can I find new ways to ease the suffering of others?

Intercession

United in love,
we gather as brothers and sisters in Christ
to pray for our own needs
and the needs of the world:

We pray for the Church and all her Christian people;
may we be guided on our journey through life
by the light of faith
towards Christ our Saviour.

Silence

Loving Father:
lead us.

We pray for those
who proclaim the Good News to the world
by word and deed;
may the Holy Spirit guide them
on their journey through life,
as they share their faith with the world.

Silence

Loving Father:
lead us.

We pray for people
forced to leave their homes and families
because of war, fear or disaster;
may they be guided
on their journey of uncertainty and suffering
by our loving support
and efforts to bring them comfort and hope.

Silence

Loving Father:
lead us.

We pray for people
wandering in the wilderness of doubt
as they search for God in their lives;
may our loving Father,
who searches for everyone who is lost,
guide them on their journey of discovery.

Silence

Loving Father:
lead us.

We pray for anyone
who has wandered far from God's love;
may they be guided on a journey
of friendship and reconciliation,
as they discover the forgiveness and healing
of our heavenly Father who never stops loving them.

Silence

Loving Father:
lead us.

Knowing that our heavenly Father is listening,
in the silence of our hearts
let us share our own unspoken prayers with him.

Silence

Heavenly Father,
as we journey through Lent,
keep us close to your love
and mould us in the image of Christ your loving Son.
We ask this in the name of Jesus our Lord.
Amen.

Activities and ideas

- Decide on a charity which the children would particularly like to support during the season of Lent. Help them to gather information about its work and aims, and produce a visual display. Encourage them to think of different ways in which they can raise funds both individually and as a group to support their chosen cause, and help them to plan and run events to achieve their aims.

- Give each child a small card cut-out in the shape of a cross with the following verse from Matthew's Gospel written or printed on one side: 'If anyone wants to come with me, he must forget himself, take up his cross and follow me.' (Matthew 16:24) Help the children to reflect about, and then write down on the other side of their cross, their private goals for their own journey through Lent. Invite them to come forward individually and touch the focal crucifix with their own crosses. They should keep these carefully as a reminder to themselves of their aims for Lent.

- Use the meditation on the Way of the Cross on pages 27-36.

Music

- Stay with me (OS)

- Follow me, follow me (LitHON/OS)

- Step by step, on and on (LitHON/OS)

- There is a green hill (OS)

- One cold night in spring (OS)

- Come and go with me (LitHON/OS)

Journey with Jesus
____ A meditation on the Way of the Cross ____

Introduction

These readings and prayers are intended to help the children to follow the footsteps of Christ's last journey to the cross, and to enter into the Passion story in a more personal way. They make the journey beside Jesus, stopping along the way to remember his suffering, but also to recall the faith and love he showed right up to the moment of his death.

In preparation for making this journey together, the children should be split into small groups and asked to prepare a visual representation or symbolic focus for each station and the resurrection (suggestions are given). These should be kept simple and numbered appropriately, so that the children can move from one to another using the relevant readings and prayers. Another group could design and make a simple banner which reads, 'Come, follow me', to be carried at the front of their procession. Depending on the space available, the symbol for each station can be placed around the crucifix or cross which forms the central focus (see page 19).

The first station   *Jesus is sentenced to death*

Focus   Coil of rope, brambles twisted to make a thorny crown.

Reading   Early the next morning, Jesus was bound and taken to Pontius Pilate, the Roman governor. Pilate questioned Jesus carefully, 'Is it true that you are the King of the Jews?' he asked. 'It is you who say this,' Jesus replied. Despite the many accusations made by the chief priests, and the questions asked by Pilate, Jesus stood silent and made no attempt to answer any of them. Reluctantly, Pilate sentenced Jesus to be crucified and handed him over to the guards.

Reflection   The prisoner said little in his own defence.
His silent acceptance and calmness
angered his accusers.
Words would make no difference anyway:
they had already agreed his guilt.

Prayer   Lord, forgive me when I fail
to recognise your presence among us;
for the times when I shut my ears and mind,
and refuse to listen to what you have to say to me.

The second station   *Jesus is crowned with thorns and receives his cross*

Focus   Simple cross made from two sticks or branches tied together.

Reading   The Roman soldiers who took charge of Jesus made fun of him and mocked 'the King of the Jews'. They wrapped him in a robe of royal purple, and plaited thorns to be his 'crown'. When they had finished taunting him, they dressed Jesus in his own clothes, and gave him a cross to carry.

Reflection   Mocked and abused,
taunted and torn,
they laughed at your misery,
and crowned your gentle head
with cruel thorns.

Prayer   Lord,
bruised and bleeding,
you accepted your lonely cross
and carried the weight of the world's sin.
Forgive me when I complain
about my own cross.
Help me to carry it gladly
on my journey through life.

The third station   *Jesus falls for the first time*

Focus   If available, use a simple wooden manikin of the
type used in art departments, to depict a falling
figure; otherwise a simple picture or 'stick' drawing
can be used or a figure made from modelling clay
or plasticine.

Reading   Exhausted and weak after being beaten and abused,
Jesus had walked only a short distance before he
stumbled under the weight of the cross, and fell
for the first time.

Reflection   The road is long
and the journey hard.
The cross grows ever heavier
and there is no one to help.
You stumble and fall.

Prayer   Lord,
how many times
have I faltered and fallen?
Tripped up by my lack of understanding,
and stumbling over pebbles of doubt.
Help me to get up
and begin again.

The fourth station   *Jesus meets his mother*

Focus

Cut-out heart, pierced with a cut-out sword, toy sword, letter opener or similar.

Reading

Many people had gathered to watch the sad procession making its way to Golgotha, and among them stood Mary, the mother of Jesus, who wept with sorrow when she saw her beloved son's suffering.

Reflection

Step by painful step
she shares your suffering,
her heart pierced by a sword of sorrow and pain.
A glance is enough,
her loving look says everything,
and then she is gone.

Prayer

Walk with me, Mary.
Stay beside me on my journey,
and comfort and strengthen me
with your mother's love.

The fifth station   *Simon helps Jesus*

Focus

Imprint of hands in damp sand or plaster; poster of handprints made with various colours of paint.

Reading

When the soldiers saw Jesus struggling, they were afraid that he would not survive the journey to the place of execution. So they chose a man from the crowd to share their prisoner's burden. The man came from Cyrene and his name was Simon. He helped Jesus to carry his heavy cross.

Reflection

A stranger in the crowd
is chosen to help you.
His hands lighten your load,
his shoulder shares your heavy burden.

Prayer

Lord,
a stranger's help
made all the difference
to your struggle.
May I help others
along the way
as they struggle
with the crosses they bear.

The sixth station   *Veronica wipes the face of Jesus*

Focus

A simple piece of white cloth with a face roughly sponged or painted in outline; or if someone doesn't mind getting messy, apply face paint and gently press a cloth against their face to create an image.

Reading

Among the crowd watching Jesus suffering was a holy woman named Veronica. Seeing his plight, she was filled with pity and compassion, and she stepped forward to gently wipe his bloodstained face with a towel. As she lifted the towel away, the image of Christ's face remained imprinted there.

Reflection

She saw your suffering
and was moved to help.
She did not stand aside,
or pass you by.
You touched each other
with love.

Prayer

Lord,
give me the courage
to step from the crowd of indifference,
and do something positive
to show my love for others.

The seventh station   *Jesus falls for the second time*

Focus

Use a similar picture or figure as the third station.

Reading

Jesus stumbled, and the weight of the cross made him fall for a second time.

Reflection

Each step grows more difficult.
The weight of your cross
seems ready to crush
as once more you fall.

Prayer

Lord, however crushed
I feel by the troubles
and worries of life,
help me to my feet,
knowing that all will be well
with you by my side.

31

The eighth station   *The women of Jerusalem weep for Jesus*

Focus

Cut out one or two large tear shapes from silver card or some plain card covered with silver foil. Give the children a selection of magazines, and help them to find and cut out pictures of people who are sad or crying. These can then be stuck on the tear shapes to make a collage.

Reading

Many of the women wept with sadness when they saw the pitiful state of Jesus as he struggled along the way to Golgotha. Seeing them crying, he said to them, 'Do not cry for me, women of Jerusalem, but save your tears for yourselves and your children.'

Reflection

The women wept for you,
but their tears made no difference
because no one would listen.

Prayer

Lord, you made time to listen,
even on your way to die.
Let me open my heart
to hear and understand
those who cry out
and are ignored.

The ninth station   *Jesus falls a third time*

Focus

As third and seventh stations.

Reading

The cross was heavy and Jesus was exhausted. Urged on by the soldiers' spears, he staggered on slowly and painfully, until finally he fell for a third time.

Reflection

Almost there now.
Not much further to go.
Face down in the dirt,
you must get up
and carry on.
Your journey is almost complete.

Prayer

Lord, don't let me give up,
when I fall time and time again.
Disheartened and feeling sorry for myself,
help me to continue on my way.

The tenth station   *Jesus is stripped of his clothes*

Focus

A pile of clothes; a couple of large dice made from covered cardboard boxes, and marked with appropriate spots.

Reading

When they reached the place of execution, the soldiers stripped Jesus and threw dice to divide his clothes among them.

Reflection

Stripped of clothes
and stripped of dignity,
standing naked before the crowd,
you suffer the final act
of humiliation.

Prayer

Lord, strip me of everything
which keeps me from being close to you
and your love.

The eleventh station   *Jesus is nailed to the cross*

Focus

Arrange a selection of the largest nails you can find, together with a mallet or hammer, next to a scroll of paper on which is written, 'Jesus of Nazareth, King of the Jews'.

Reading

When they reached the place called 'the skull', they nailed Jesus to the cross and raised it up to stand between two thieves. Above him they placed a sign which read, 'Jesus of Nazareth, King of the Jews'.

Reflection

They pierced
your gentle hands and feet,
and nailed you to the wood.
Stretched out in love,
you hang above the world
you came to save.

Prayer

King of love,
forgive me when I wound
and hurt you
by turning away
from your outstretched arms.

33

The twelfth station   *Jesus dies on the cross*

Focus   A crucifix or cross with a piece of black cloth draped over it.

Reading   For three hours darkness fell over the land like a blanket, and the sun lost its brightness. Then Jesus called out, 'My God, my God, why have you abandoned me?' And a short time later he cried out again, 'Father, I place my spirit into your loving hands.' Then he bowed his head and died.

Reflection   You hang there lifeless.
Your task is finally complete.
Your journey has finished.

Prayer   Lord,
when everything seems lost,
and darkness surrounds us,
may we look at your cross
and be filled with hope.

The thirteenth station   *Jesus is taken down from the cross*

Focus   Lay a plasticine figure on a brick or piece of rock or stone, and drape a cloth over the 'body'.

Reading   Joseph of Arimathea, who was a disciple of Jesus, asked Pilate for permission to remove his body from the cross. Together with Nicodemus, he gently lifted Jesus down and placed him in the arms of Mary his loving mother.

Reflection   Once more you are held
in the loving arms
which first held you
in a stable long ago,
and wrapped you
in a lifetime of love.

Prayer   Lord,
like Mary your mother
may I welcome you
into my life
with open arms.

34

The fourteenth station

Jesus is laid in the tomb

Focus

With a little imagination there are many different ways to create a tomb scene depending on the time and resources available – for example, a 'living garden' in a tray or bowl, something constructed from papier-mâché, or a simple collection of suitably arranged stones.

Reading

Joseph and Nicodemus wrapped Jesus in a shroud, and, together with the women, they carried his body to the tomb where he was to be buried. They laid him inside and rolled a stone against the entrance.

Reflection

They left you covered
and alone
in the darkness of the tomb,
and the darkness of sorrow.

Prayer

Lord,
let your tomb
be a symbol of hope and joy
in moments of sadness and sorrow.

Resurrection

Jesus is alive!

Focus

A large candle or resurrection cross, covered with fresh or paper flowers, can be used to represent the joy of Easter.

Reading

Before sunrise on the Sunday morning, Mary of Magdala went to the tomb. As she reached the entrance, she saw that the stone had been rolled away and the tomb was empty. She ran to the disciples, saying, 'They have taken the Lord from the tomb and we don't know where they have put him!' Peter and another disciple, John, ran to the tomb and found it just as Mary had described, with the linen burial cloths lying on the ground. The cloth which had been wrapped around Jesus' head lay rolled up separately from the other pieces of cloth. Peter went into the tomb first, followed by John.

Until this moment they had not understood the Scriptures, which had said, 'He must rise from the dead.' But now they saw, and they believed.

Reflection   The cloths which bound you
have been cast off with death.
A new day dawns,
a new life rises
to greet the world.

Prayer   Lord,
may the glory of your resurrection
and the promise of eternal life
fill my lifelong journey
with hope and joy.

3

Thanks for the harvest

Focus

Arrange an assortment of flowers, harvest fruits and produce around a central candle and a Bible opened at Leviticus 26:4-5. Add any suitable pictures or symbols of 'creation'.

Introduction

God created the world and all its wonders for us to use and enjoy, and he provides for all our needs. Nowadays few of us grow our own food or have to spend much time worrying about where our next meal will come from. But, traditionally, people have remembered God's loving care and goodness at harvest time, and thanked him for continuing to provide for our needs by sharing with others what we have so generously been given.

Penitential reflection

Lord of creation,
for the times we have taken
your gifts of love for granted:
Lord, have mercy.
Lord, have mercy.

Lord of creation,
for the times when we have put our own needs
before those of others:
Christ, have mercy.
Christ, have mercy.

Lord of creation,
for the times when we have been selfish
and unwilling to share:
Lord, have mercy.
Lord, have mercy.

Scripture   *Old Testament reading – adapted from Leviticus 26:4-5*

God said, 'I will send rain to water the earth and produce a rich harvest. Trees will bend under the weight of their fruit, and fields overflow with corn and every kind of crop. You will have as much food as you can eat, and be filled with contentment and happiness.'

Litany of thanksgiving – adapted from Psalm 135

You moulded the earth,
and set the sun in the sky.
Thank you, God, for all your goodness.

You filled the seas with life,
and sprinkled the heavens with stars.
Thank you, God, for all your goodness.

You made the darkness bright,
and breathed life into creation.
Thank you, God, for all your goodness.

You feed each living creature,
and your love is unending.
Thank you, God, for all your goodness.

Gospel – adapted from Mark 4:26-29

Jesus said to his disciples, 'Think of a man who scatters seed in his field. Hour by hour, through daylight and darkness, the seeds send out shoots and roots, and begin to grow. The man does not know how this all happens, but before long his field is full of crops, and when the harvest is ripe, the man begins to reap what he has sown.'

Reflection   (If possible, begin by playing a recording of 'What a wonderful world' by Louis Armstrong.)

At the end of the creation story, the book of Genesis tells us that 'God looked at everything he had made and saw that it was very good' (Genesis 1:31). What is amazing, perhaps, is that God wanted to share his marvellous creation with us, and entrust such a very special gift, so lovingly crafted, to our human care. God provides everything that is necessary for his creation to continue to be fruitful and multiply. Nature's miracles happen every day, but often we simply forget to look around us and take note of the wonderful world created by God. Unless we are careful, we can take the seasons of the year, the life-giving sun and rain, and the way in which everything grows very much for granted, and we forget to marvel at God's wonderful work.

When someone gives us a gift, we show our appreciation first by remembering to thank them, and then by the way in which we take care of that gift. When we choose to use litter bins and to recycle things rather than waste them unnecessarily, then our efforts to protect the environment are all ways of thanking God for creation. When people show no respect for the world or its living creatures, then they also show no respect for the One who created them.

God takes care of all our needs and provides enough food for the whole world. There are places and countries which suffer from famine or food shortages because of natural or man-made disasters. But there are many ways we can help people at times of crisis if we are prepared to share what we are fortunate enough to have.

So, once a year, as summer draws to a close and the crops of the field are safely gathered in before the winter, it is good to make time to thank God for the harvest and his generous gifts of creation. It is also a time to think about those who are less fortunate, and remind ourselves of our responsibility to share what we have with others.

Intercession As we remember God's love for us,
let us pray in the Spirit of Christ
for the needs of the world:

Let us pray to the God of creation
that we will cherish and respect his world,
taking care to use its resources wisely,
and avoiding pollution and unnecessary waste.

Silence

Lord, in your mercy:
hear our prayer.

Let us pray to the God of creation
that the destruction of war will belong to the past,
through our efforts
to encourage peace and forgiveness.

Silence

Lord, in your mercy:
hear our prayer.

Let us pray to the God of creation
that hunger will be satisfied and poverty destroyed,
as countries which have plenty
share their resources and technology
with those which have little.

Silence

Lord, in your mercy:
hear our prayer.

Let us pray to the God of creation
that we will always respect and protect his gift of life,
remembering to treat one another with the dignity
which every person created in God's image deserves.

Silence

Lord, in your mercy:
hear our prayer.

Knowing that our heavenly Father is listening,
in the silence of our hearts
let us share our own unspoken prayers with him.

Silence

All-powerful God,
Creator of all living things,
your gifts of love bring us life and joy.
Help us always to treasure and appreciate
what we have so generously been given.
We make our prayers
through Jesus Christ your only Son.
Amen.

Activities and ideas

- In preparation for their harvest celebration, the children can make harvest gift boxes to be filled with food items and shared with those in need. You will need card or cardboard, a selection of wool or string, sellotape, scissors, a ruler and pencil, and a safety knife and suitable surface on which to cut the card. Make a cross-shaped template of whatever size you choose, and use this to draw identical outlines on pieces of card. When selecting dimensions, remember that the central square will form the base of your finished basket and give you a good idea of the overall size of the completed article. Use scissors to cut around the template outline, and carefully score and bend the card along the edges of the central square before folding up the sides of the box. On three of the four sides, cut out four narrow wedge shapes to leave five 'fingers' of card. On the remaining fourth side, cut out five wedges. Choose a length of coloured wool, and carefully tape one end in a corner before beginning to weave around the strips of card. Take care to pull the wool tight as you weave, and draw the sides of the box up as you go. Tie or tape new lengths of different coloured wool in place as you continue weaving until you complete the box. Each child can fill their box with various foodstuffs to be given as gifts.

- Give the children a selection of magazines and ask them to create a collage using pictures of food which can be mounted as a banner or display. Add the heading: God fills our world with food to share.

- Instead of giving individual gift boxes, create several larger 'hampers' by covering or decorating cardboard boxes. The children can be invited to come forward during the celebration and place their own gift or gifts in the hampers.

- As the weather turns colder, encourage the children to think about the needs of some of God's other creatures by helping them to make 'cake' for the wild birds. You will need yoghurt pots, string, scissors, lard, a saucepan, a mixing bowl, spoons and a selection of suitable scraps – for example, breadcrumbs, peanuts (unsalted), chopped apple, dried fruit such as currants or raisins, bacon rind, stale cake or biscuits which have been crumbed. Carefully make a hole in the bottom of each yoghurt pot, and thread a length of string through. Make a large knot in the end of the string inside the pot, making sure that it cannot be pulled through the hole. Place the scraps in a mixing bowl, and carefully pour on the lard which has been melted in a saucepan over a gentle heat. (This should only be done by an adult!) Stir the mixture to thoroughly coat all the ingredients with lard, before carefully spooning it into the yoghurt pots and pressing down firmly. Leave the pots to cool until the lard has hardened, before turning the pots upside down and hanging them outside for the birds.

• At the time of this celebration, if there is an appropriate appeal for famine relief or similar in the news, encourage the children to find out more by gathering information and finding out details of stories behind the headlines and any relief agencies which are involved. Help them to come up with their own ideas about how they can contribute to these relief efforts. Alternatively, there are several different schemes for sponsoring children in underdeveloped parts of the world. The children could support one of these, and actually make contact with another child or children who would benefit from their fund-raising efforts. Remember, though, that this requires long-term commitment.

Music

• 'Feed the world' by Band Aid (similar songs can be useful discussion starters)

• He's got the whole world in his hand (LitHON/OS)

• O Lord, all the world belongs to you (LitHON/OS)

• Morning has broken (LitHON/OS)

• All things bright and beautiful (LitHON/OS)

• Push, little seed (OS)

• We eat the plants that grow from seed (OS)

4

Serving one another
(Celebrating new beginnings)

Focus
A Bible open at John's account of the washing of feet in Chapter 13; a towel and a bowl of water; a large candle; all encircled by individual nightlights (unlit). If possible, have a copy of Sieger Koder's *The washing of feet* on display.*

Introduction
Jesus constantly showed us how to serve God and one another by his loving example. We have been created in his image to love others just as he loves us. As we gather together to celebrate the beginning of this new school term/year, let us reflect together on the importance of treating one another with the love, forgiveness and respect which show the world that we are indeed Christ's disciples.

Penitential reflection
Jesus said, 'Whatever you do to the least of my brothers or sisters, you do to me.' (Matthew 25:40)

When we have failed to see God in others:
Lord of forgiveness:
have mercy on us.

When we have failed to let God into our daily lives:
Lord of love:
have mercy on us.

When we have failed to follow
your commandments of love:
Lord of life:
have mercy on us.

* Details are available from St Paul Multimedia Productions, Middle Green, Slough SL3 6BS (tel 01753 577629; fax 01753 511809)

Scripture   *New Testament reading – adapted from Romans 12:4-5, 8-11, 18*

Just as our bodies have many parts each with a different function, in the same way, although we are many, we make up one body in Christ, and each of us has an important part to play. Give generously to one another; if someone asks you to do something, do it to the best of your ability; let the kindness and forgiveness you show to one another be genuinely heartfelt. Think of the needs of others before your own, and let your actions and attitudes express the love and care you feel. Work hard and always try your very best at whatever you do. Above all else, try to please God, and be at peace with one another.

Psalm – adapted from Psalm 138:1-6, 8, 9, 11

Lord, you know me through and through.
You know when I sit and when I stand.
You know each thought I think and move I make.
You know everything I do.

Wherever I am, you are there.

Before I speak you know what I will say.
You hold me in your loving hands.
Your greatness is beyond my understanding.
Wherever I am, you are there.

Wherever I am, you are there.

If I climb the highest hill, you are there.
If I journey east or west, you are there.
If the darkness covers me, you are there beside me.
Your light turns the night to day.

Wherever I am, you are there.

For you created and formed me.
Inside my mother, you gave me life.
I thank you for the wonder of me.
I thank you for the wonders of you.

Wherever I am, you are there.

Gospel – adapted from Mark 10:43-45

Jesus said to them, 'Anyone who wants to be great must be ready to serve everyone else; anyone who wants to be first must be ready to put others before them. After all, the Son of Man came to serve others, and to give up his life to set many people free.'

Gospel – adapted from John 13:1-15, 34-35

(If possible, the words of Jesus and Peter should be read by different voices.)

It was just before the Passover celebration, and, knowing that the time for him to die was fast approaching, Jesus showed his disciples the depth of his love for them.

While they were at supper together, Jesus stood up and, laying his outer garments to one side, he wrapped a towel around his waist. The disciples watched as he fetched a basin of water and knelt down to wash their feet one by one, before drying them with the towel. When it was Peter's turn, he protested loudly, 'Lord, it isn't right that you should wash my feet!' But gently Jesus insisted, and reluctantly Peter allowed his Master to wash his feet. When he had finished, Jesus dressed and returned to the table. 'Just as your Lord and Master has washed your feet, so you must be ready to do for others what I have done for you.' Then he told them, 'This is my new commandment: love one another as I have loved you. The world will know that you are my disciples by the love you have for one another.'

Reflection

Jesus chose a dramatic and powerful way to demonstrate to his followers exactly how he expects us to treat one another. We are left in no doubt that we are called to serve one another, whatever our position in life might be. His role as servant made the disciples feel extremely uncomfortable, and we heard how Peter objected loudly to having his feet washed by his Master. It is a gesture and scene

CELEBRATIONS FOR YOUNG PEOPLE

which we remember and re-enact at the Mass of the Lord's Supper on Holy Thursday, which makes us feel humbled and deeply touched as we are reminded of Christ's remarkable love for us.

But serving one another calls for more than simply washing one another's feet. Think for a moment about some of the people who have served you recently – at home, at school, out shopping or perhaps on holiday. How did you react to what they said and did for you? How did you treat them?

As you begin a new school term/year, your teachers, your friends and your families will find an enormous number of ways to be of service to you. How will you respond to their gestures and efforts? With thanks and appreciation for their hard work, and by making your own special efforts to express your love and care for those around you? Often it is easy to take the efforts of others for granted, and we forget to say thank you. We can be oblivious to the amount of time and preparation which those around us put in just to make our everyday lives run smoothly. This can range from having our sandwiches made for school, or clean uniform ready when we need it, to the preparation a teacher makes before each lesson. Unless we are careful, it is easier to criticise than to appreciate.

Serving one another is one way in which Jesus expects us to show our love for others. It is a commandment which Christ himself gave us. In every act of love and service offered in every home, workplace, kitchen and canteen, school or playground, we wash the feet of one another. It is something which we are all called to do; it is the 'hallmark' of every Christian. 'By your love for one another everyone will recognise you as my disciples.'

It is this love which is given, received and shared in our individual lives that we celebrate together in the Eucharist. In this way, though we are many parts in the one body of Christ, as children of God we may 'Go in peace to love and serve the Lord.'

Intercession   Father, we come before you in love
to ask you to listen to the prayers of your children:

We pray that as Christians
we will serve God and one another
by becoming instruments of love in God's hands,
by feeding the hungry, clothing the naked
and befriending the homeless and unwanted.

Silence

Lord of love:
help us to serve you.

We pray that we will be encouraged and inspired
by the lives of the Saints
and all who dedicate their lives
to sharing and living the Gospel of love,
to do God's holy will.

Silence

Lord of love:
help us to serve you.

We pray that we will satisfy
our neighbour's hunger for love
by giving them a smile, sharing a glass of water,
or simply making time to talk and listen.

Silence

Lord of love:
help us to serve you.

We pray that God will give us
the strength and courage
to allow ourselves to go wherever he sends us,
and to do whatever he asks.

Silence

Lord of love:
help us to serve you.

We pray that our eyes will open
to see Christ in the faces of our neighbours,
and our hearts will open to respond lovingly
to their needs.

Silence

Lord of love:
help us to serve you.

Knowing that our heavenly Father is listening,
in the silence of our hearts
let us share our own unspoken prayers with him.

Silence

Lord God,
you sent your beloved Son
to be our Servant King,
and to teach us your loving ways.
Fill us with the Holy Spirit,
and help us to serve you and one another,
according to your commandments of love.
We make our prayers through Christ our Lord.
Amen.

Activities and ideas

- Dramatise the Gospel scene as read or transpose it to a modern situation. If possible, use a mixture of adults and children to emphasise that we should serve one another regardless of age or status.

- Encourage the children to suggest ways in which we can 'wash one another's feet' by expressing our love for one another. Write their ideas on a large sheet of paper for all to see.

- You will need pieces of fringed paper which represent small towels and coloured felt-tips or pencils. Give each child a paper 'towel', and after a moment of reflection ask them to write down one way in which they can serve another person by a loving gesture or action. They can then decorate the other side of the towel. Collect in the pieces of paper and arrange them on the central display or focus. At an appropriate point in your celebration, invite each child to come forward and collect a paper towel (not their own), before returning to their place with the suggestion they have received for serving others.

- Sing together 'A new commandment'. Then invite the children to spend a few quiet moments reflecting on ways in which they can put Christ's commandment into practice this term/year. Then invite each person to light one of the smaller nightlights from the large candle.

- It might be possible to find some way of serving someone in the local community. This could involve raising funds or supporting a particular group or charity, or it could take the form of more hands-on involvement in a local community project or scheme in which some or all of the children could participate.

Music
- This is my body (LitHON/OS)
- A new commandment (LitHON/OS)
- Yahweh, I know you are near (LitHON/OS)
- Lord, the light of your love (Shine, Jesus, shine) (LitHON/OS)
- Will you come and follow me (LitHON)

5
Joy and thanksgiving
_____ (Celebrating the past we've shared) _____

Focus   Place a crucifix on a brightly coloured piece of fabric, together with a large candle or 'Christ light'. Scatter fresh flowers around the display.

Introduction   As the end of another school term/year approaches, and we look forward with joy and excitement to a well-deserved holiday and break from our every-day routine, it is good to stop for a moment and make time to remember the good times we have shared, and to give thanks to God, and our teachers, parents and friends for all their loving support and encouragement.

Penitential reflection   For the times when we have let one another down by our words or actions:
Lord, forgive us.
Lord, forgive us.

For the times when we wandered away
from God's path of truth and forgiveness:
Christ, forgive us.
Christ, forgive us.

For the times when we have ignored
God's presence in our lives:
Lord, forgive us.
Lord, forgive us.

Scripture   *New Testament reading – adapted from Philippians 1:3-6*

Every time I think of you I give thanks to God; and every prayer I make for you is filled with joy because you have shared the Gospel from the very first moment you heard it. I know that God will carry on working in you until Christ our Lord returns.

Gospel – adapted from John 16:16, 20, 22, 24

Jesus said to his disciples, 'In a while I will leave you, but soon afterwards we will meet again. You will cry with sadness while others give thanks, but your sorrow will not last long and will quickly turn to the kind of joy which no one can ever spoil. Until now, you have asked for nothing in my name, but whatever you ask for you will receive to make your happiness complete.'

Gospel – adapted from Matthew 28:1-8

At sunrise on the Sunday morning, Mary of Magdala and another woman called Mary went to the tomb where Jesus was buried. Suddenly the ground trembled violently like an earthquake, and an angel appeared, rolled the stone away from the tomb and sat on it. The angel dazzled like lightning, and the guards at the tomb were frozen with fear. Then the angel spoke to the women, saying, 'Do not be afraid! I know that you are looking for Jesus, who was crucified and buried here, but you will not find him because he is risen, just as he told you. Come and see for yourselves that he is gone! Now you must go to his disciples and tell them that he is risen, and you will see him again in Galilee. Go, and remember everything I have told you.'

Overwhelmed with joy and excitement, the two women hurried from the tomb, and ran to tell the disciples their marvellous news.

Reflection

Often when people look back over their lives, they find that the happy memories they have far out-number the sad ones. 'The summers seemed longer and the sun always shone when we were young!' you'll often hear them remark, as they recall their childhood days. Perhaps this is simply because nature seems to have a way of making bad mem-ories fade more quickly with the passage of time, leaving the good ones for us to treasure and enjoy. That is why so many older people are quick to tell you that 'your school years are the best years of your life'. They forget the pressures of homework and exams, and the complications of falling in and out of friendship which are often a part of ordinary school life. Time will tell whether you agree with them or not!

As the time for him to die approached, Jesus tried to warn his disciples that sad and difficult times lay ahead for them, while reassuring them that any sorrow would quickly be replaced by a sense of joy which would remain within their hearts for ever. The disciples failed to understand that Jesus was referring to his own death and resurrection. Soon afterwards, just as he had foretold, the desperate sense of despair and sadness, which threatened to overwhelm them at his crucifixion and death, were replaced by incredible joy as they realised that he had risen from the dead and was indeed alive. Even when he finally ascended to his heavenly Father, they had their precious memories and stories to treasure and share with the world through the New Testament accounts of Christ's life and teaching.

The joy and sense of celebration the apostles experienced and shared that first Easter remain at the very hearts of our Christian lives today. Every Sunday we gather as one family, to rejoice at Christ's resurrection and victory over death, and to give thanks for his gift of eternal life. We carry that joy with us in our hearts, and take it out to the world to share with one another in our ordinary everyday lives.

So today let's celebrate and give thanks for all the fun and good times we have enjoyed and shared together as a community. Any difficulties and problems we might have experienced this term/year, will quickly fade with time as we leave such things in the past where they belong. May this break refresh and renew us and prepare us to make a fresh start at the beginning of next term, as we take our joy out to share with the world until we meet again.

Intercession
Gathered together in love,
as brothers and sisters in Christ,
let us ask our loving Father
to listen to the prayers we make.

Let us pray for children
and their families everywhere
at holiday time;
may we give thanks
for the precious time we share together.

Silence

Lord, in your love:
fill us with joy.

Let us pray for the gifts of creation;
may we give thanks to God for every living thing,
and take care to protect and care for his world.

Silence

Lord, in your love:
fill us with joy.

Let us pray for people who care for the sick;
may we give thanks for their skill
and for the love of those
who look after us at times of illness.

Silence

Lord, in your love:
fill us with joy.

Let us pray for all who rest in peace with God;
may we give thanks that Jesus died and rose again,
so that we can live happily with him
for ever in heaven.

Silence

Lord, in your love:
fill us with joy.

Let us pray for people who are alone
and filled with despair;
may we give thanks that our friendship and love
can fill their lives with the joy and hope we share.

Silence

Lord, in your love:
fill us with joy.

Let us pray for our families and friends;
may we give thanks for loving homes
and the precious gift of friendship.

Silence

Lord, in your love:
fill us with joy.

Knowing that our heavenly Father is listening,
in the silence of our hearts
let us share our own unspoken prayers with him.

Silence

Loving Father,
you fill our lives with joy
in your wonderful world.
Help us to share all that you give us,
so that we can make this world
a happier place for everyone to live.
Grant this through Christ your Son.
Amen.

Activities and ideas
- Ask the children to write an account or draw a picture of their own favourite event or memory for the term or year. If possible, mount these on a display, together with any relevant photographs you might have. The display should be colourful and eye-catching, and displayed in an accessible

position where children, parents and staff have the opportunity to look at and read what has been prepared.

• Arrange the children in a circle (this can be more than one row). Ask one of the children to light a smaller candle (which can be safely carried) from the Christ light on the focal display, and place it on the floor in the centre of the group. Play an appropriate piece of music as the children listen to the Scripture passage from chapter 16 of John's Gospel. Pass the candle carefully around the group, inviting each child to hold it and, silently or aloud, pray about something or someone they would like to thank God for.

• You will need a piece of paper and a pen or pencil for each child. Give the children 5-10 minutes to reflect on the people in their lives who help to make them happy. Ask them to write down their names and carefully fold up their pieces of paper. With quiet music playing in the background, invite them to place their pieces of paper around the crucifix on the central focus as they bring those people to Christ's love. When each child has returned to his or her place, ask them to hold hands as you pray together:

Litany of thanksgiving

For our friends and families:
we thank you, Lord.

For laughter and love:
we thank you, Lord.

For joy in our hearts:
we thank you, Lord.

For everyone who cares for us:
we thank you, Lord.

For peace in our lives:
we thank you, Lord.

Pause for a moment of silence before singing 'Give me joy in my heart' together.

- You will need folded pieces of plain or coloured card, pens or pencils for colouring, an assortment of materials such as sequins or glitter. Encourage the children to think of someone who especially deserves their thanks. It might be a friend, a parent, a teacher, a neighbour or acquaintance, or Jesus. Ask them to design and decorate a thank-you card to give as a token of their appreciation for that special person.

Music
- Give me joy in my heart (LitHON/OS)
- Colours of day (LitHON/OS)
- You shall go out with joy (LitHON/OS)
- Rejoice in the Lord always (LitHON/OS)
- Jesus put this song into our hearts (LitHON/OS)

6

Peace

Focus

Arrange pieces of driftwood, shells, gravel and/or stones on some sand around a candle and a picture or icon of Jesus.

Introduction

Jesus said to his disciples, 'Peace is my gift to you, my own peace I give to you, a peace that the world cannot give.' (John 14:29)

Jesus is our peace. He overcomes division and hatred with love and forgiveness. As Christians we are called to love one another as Christ loves us and to share his very special gift of peace with the world in which we live.

Penitential reflection

Jesus said, 'If you are about to come before God to pray, and then remember that you have quarrelled with someone, first go away, settle your argument and make your peace with them.' (Matthew 5:23-26)

If we have hurt anyone by our words or actions:
Lord, have mercy.
Lord, have mercy.

If we have ignored someone
and made them feel unloved:
Christ, have mercy.
Christ, have mercy.

If we have been unforgiving and filled with anger:
Lord, have mercy.
Lord, have mercy.

Scripture   *Old Testament reading – adapted from 1 Kings 19:8, 11-13*

When the prophet Elijah reached Horeb, the mountain of God, he spent the night in a cave and the Word of God came to him there. He was told to leave the shelter of the cave and stand on the mountainside before the Lord. As Elijah stood at the cave entrance, there came a mighty storm, as powerful and destructive as a hurricane. But God was not in the storm. Next the earth shook, and the mountain quaked beneath Elijah's feet. But God was not in the earthquake. After the earthquake came a scorching fire, but God was not in the fire either. Then, finally, Elijah heard the sound of a gentle breeze blowing through the trees, and he covered his face and went out to meet the Lord God.

Gospel – adapted from Mark 4:35-41

Jesus and his disciples set off to sail to the other side of the Sea of Galilee. Jesus had been preaching all day, and feeling tired, he was soon lulled to sleep by the rocking of the boat. Suddenly a storm blew up, and great waves began to pound the boat. The disciples were terrified and ran to waken Jesus before they all drowned. Hearing their cries, Jesus got up and scolded the sea and wind with the words, 'Be at peace!'

At once the wind dropped and the sea grew calm again. Then Jesus asked his disciples, 'Why were you so afraid? Did you not believe in me?' They were filled with wonder because they had seen that even the sea and wind would obey his commands.

Reflection   (Read the text very slowly, pausing at full stops for as much as five seconds. Make sure that your voice is calm and slow. Allow several minutes of silence at the end of the reflection).

Our lives are noisy places where the sound of silence is rarely heard.

(Play recorded sound track – see Activities and ideas section.)

I want you to close your eyes. Take a deep breath . . . and relax.

Imagine it is a warm summer's day and you are sitting in a garden.

Feel the warmth of the sunshine on your face and the softness of the grass beneath your body.

Smell the sweet scent of the roses growing nearby.

Listen. What can you hear? *(Pause)*

There is a soft, warm breeze blowing. All around you, the leaves on the trees gently rustle as they dance to its tune. You cannot see the wind. It has no colour or form, but you can feel its touch on your face and hear it moving through the stillness around you.

Suddenly your moment of peace is shattered by the roar of traffic; the sound of voices; a barking dog; banging doors; a distant siren.

The hum-drum bustle of everyday life has destroyed the calm.

But listen again. What can you hear?

Among the noise and distractions, the wind is still blowing gently. It had never stopped. *(Pause)*

Now slowly open your eyes.

Elijah recognised the power of God not in a mighty wind, a powerful earthquake, or a raging fire, but in the peace and stillness of a gentle breeze. God moves through our lives like a gentle breeze which we don't always notice. He is constantly there in the background, even when other distractions divert our attention, and the noise in our busy daily lives seems to drown out his peaceful presence.

The disciples recognised the power of Jesus in his ability to calm the storm and still the troubled waters which threatened to sink them. Just as he heard their cries for help, at stormy moments in our lives, when perhaps we feel unhappy, worried, or

things simply don't seem to be going very well,
Jesus will restore our calmness and peace. In times
of trouble and uncertainty, we can call out and ask
Jesus to make things right again.

Intercession

Jesus told us to come to him like little children
with all our worries and troubles.
Let us pray now for our own needs
and the needs of our world:

We pray for the Church
and everyone who belongs to its family;
may we share the Gospel of peace
by our living example of acceptance, understanding
and forgiveness.

Silence

Lord God:
grant us your peace.

We pray for peacemakers in our world;
may we support their brave efforts to heal injustice,
and to reconcile differences and bitterness
in countries and communities
divided by fear and hatred.

Silence

Lord God:
grant us your peace.

We pray for those
who are filled with doubt and uncertainty;
may they find faith in Jesus the risen Lord,
and be filled with the gift of his peace.

Silence

Lord God:
grant us your peace.

We pray for families and homes
broken and damaged by violence and anger;

may they discover the healing peace of Christ
through our loving help,
and find the strength and courage
to rebuild their lives.

Silence

Lord God:
grant us your peace.

Knowing that our heavenly Father is listening,
in the silence of our hearts
let us share our own unspoken prayers with him.

Silence

God our Father,
you sent your beloved Son Jesus
who is the Prince of Peace,
to transform our world with his love.
May our living love
touch the lives of others,
and bring them the gift of your peace.
We make our prayers through Christ our Lord
Amen.

Activities and ideas

- Using suggestions made by the children, prepare a tape recording of familiar sounds, noises, and background distractions in our everyday lives – for example, telephone ringing, television, people talking, music/radio, traffic noise, doorbell. This can be played at the beginning of the reflection.

- Make a moving model of the storm scene which can be used to illustrate the Gospel story. Cut out a boat and figures from card, and firmly attach a stick (lollipop sticks or kebab sticks with their sharp ends removed) at each end. Place a table on its side and cover the table top with blue paper or material. A stormy backdrop can be hung behind. A puppeteer can kneel behind the table out of view to move the boat as it's tossed on the stormy sea. Children on each side of the table can use lengths of blue fabric to represent the sea.

- Use extracts of recorded music (see suggestions below) to add atmosphere, or alternatively make your own background sounds using rice or dried pulses in plastic bottles. Allow adequate time to practise the actions and suitable sound effects which accompany the Gospel.

- Use images and headlines from magazines and newspapers to design and create a collage display which compares and contrasts peaceful and stormy times in people's lives. Display this in a prominent position during the celebration.

- Act out the first reading or Gospel as a short drama or mime which can be performed to music.

Music
- Mendelssohn: *Fingal's Cave*

- Wagner: *The Ride of the Valkyries*

- Khachaturian: Adagio from *Spartacus* (*Onedin Line* theme tune)

- 'The sound of silence' by Simon and Garfunkel

- Listen, let your heart keep seeking (LitHON/OS)

- Be still, for the presence of the Lord (LitHON/OS)

- O, the love of my Lord (LitHON/OS)

- Peace, perfect peace, is the gift (LitHON/OS)

- Give me peace, O Lord (LitHON/OS)

- With Jesus in the boat (OS)

- Peace I leave with you (LitHON/OS)

7

Forgiveness and reconciliation

Focus
: In a central position, arrange a large crucifix and a selection of candles on a brightly coloured background cloth.

Introduction
: God loves us so much that he forgives all our mistakes. Lovingly he watches and waits, hoping that when we choose to wander away from his love, we will one day turn back to him, longing for forgiveness and full of hope and determination to make a fresh start, a new beginning.

Penitential reflection
: When we have allowed angry words to hurt and divide us:
Lord, forgive us.
Lord, forgive us.

When we have chosen the way that is not God's way:
Christ, forgive us.
Christ, forgive us.

When we have been quick to judge
and unforgiving towards each other:
Lord, forgive us.
Lord, forgive us.

Scripture
: *New Testament reading – adapted from 1 Corinthians 13:4-7, 13*

Love is patient and kind; it is not jealous or full of self-importance; love is not selfish or greedy; it does not anger easily or remember past mistakes; love finds no joy in what is wrong, but delights in what is right. Love is always trusting; hoping in the future and accepting whatever it might bring.

Many things may come and go, but love will never end.

There are three important things: faith, hope and love, and the greatest of these is love.

Psalm – adapted from Psalm 102

God is tender and forgiving,
slow to anger and rich in patience.
We can depend on his steadfast love
which nothing can ever change.

God is compassion and love.

He holds no mistakes against us,
nor remembers the times when we let him down.
Nothing can make him love us any less,
because he is our Father and we are his children.

God is compassion and love.

Gospel – adapted from John 8:1-11

Jesus was teaching in the Temple when the Pharisees brought a woman to stand before him. 'This woman has been caught breaking the Law, and the punishment for her offence is death by stoning,' they said. 'What do you have to say?' they asked, because they wanted to test Jesus.

Jesus bent down and began writing something on the ground with his finger. Again, they put their question to him. After a few moments Jesus stood up and said, 'Let the person who has never done anything wrong throw the first stone at her.' And he continued writing as before.

The crowd that had gathered began to leave one by one, until Jesus and the woman stood alone. Then Jesus said to her, 'Has anyone found you guilty?' 'No, sir,' she answered. 'Then neither do I,' he said. 'Now go and sin no more.'

Reflection

'Love' is a word we use in so many different ways about so many different things. We 'love' certain television programmes or songs. We 'love' to play certain computer games or to go shopping. We 'love' to eat a McDonald's or to play football. And yet the word 'love' is one which most of us seldom use with one another. When was the last time you told someone that you loved them, and really meant it?

There is someone who loves us unconditionally in spite of what we say and do. That someone is God. In the first reading we heard St Paul describing some of the qualities of true or genuine love. It is not always easy to love one another, and yet that is what Jesus commanded us to do: 'Love one another as I have loved you' (John 13:34). So great was Christ's love that he poured out his life on the cross for the forgiveness of our sins.

It is because of this enormous love for us that God forgives us before we have even asked to be forgiven. Love and forgiveness belong together and cannot exist apart. We can only discover the gift of God's forgiveness and peace when we choose to live in his love.

But it is not enough simply to ask God for forgiveness; we must also be ready to forgive one another. Christ taught us to pray, 'Forgive us our trespasses as we forgive those who trespass against us.' Jesus did not condemn the sinner, but the sin which they had committed. His forgiveness changed the life of the sinful woman and allowed her to be accepted into the community again. He expects us to offer forgiveness to others as readily as we receive it for ourselves.

Just like the crowd that gathered to condemn the woman, we are all guilty of judging others; of finding the splinter in the eye of someone else, without seeing the tree-trunk in our own! It is much easier to point out the faults of others than to admit to our own failings. Unless we are careful, we can all carry 'stones' of judgement which can be directed at those who need forgiveness and compassion, instead of condemnation.

And just like the woman who stood surrounded by the crowd, we all make mistakes in our lives and do things we later regret. Without the forgiveness of others, we too can expect to feel the 'stones' of intolerance and judgement directed towards us.

'Lord may you forgive us our trespasses as we forgive those who trespass against us.'

Intercession

God loved the world so much
he sent his only beloved Son
to bring his forgiveness and save us from sin.
Confident in such love,
let us pray for our needs and the needs of our world:

We bring to God's forgiving love
the Church and her people;
we pray that people
who have turned away from him
may rediscover the path which leads to his love.

Silence

Lord of forgiveness:
lead us back to your love.

We bring to God's forgiving love
nations and people who are divided
by hatred and conflict;
we pray that the power of his love
will make us forgiving towards one another,
just as he is forgiving towards us.

Silence

Lord of forgiveness:
lead us back to your love.

We bring to God's forgiving love
people in prison
and the families who suffer with them;
we pray that as Christians we may offer compassion
instead of judgement,
and give them the opportunity
to leave their mistakes in the past
and make a fresh start.

Silence

Lord of forgiveness:
lead us back to your love.

We bring to God's forgiving love
those whose hearts and lives are so filled
with resentment and anger
that there is little room for forgiveness;
we pray that he will heal their hardened hearts
and transform their lives with love.

Silence

Lord of forgiveness:
lead us back to your love.

Knowing that our heavenly Father is listening,
in the silence of our hearts
let us share our own unspoken prayers with him.

Silence

Forgiving Father,
you are full of mercy and compassion;
mould us in your image,
and help us to become people of forgiveness,
so that we may grow closer to you.
Grant this through Christ our Lord.
Amen.

Activities and ideas

• *Liturgy of forgiveness*

This can be used as an opportunity for different age groups of children to come together. The older children could act out the mime while the younger children take responsibility for preparing the symbolic crosses and gathering sufficient quantities of stones for everyone.

Collect some twigs or small branches and cut them into short lengths, or use cocktail sticks with the sharp ends removed. Show the children how to bind two pieces of wood together to make a cross, using a short length of twine or thread (or use the wire fasteners used to secure sandwich bags). If preferred, make crosses from card which the children can decorate. Place the little crosses in a basket or suitable container. In addition, ask each child to find a stone and carefully wash and dry it. (They will need more than one each if they are collecting for other children as well.) Encourage them to examine their particular stone carefully. Is it smooth or rough? Does it have any sharp or uneven edges? What colour is it? Are any of the stones they have collected exactly the same? Again, collect these together in a basket or suitable container.

Gather the children around the crucifix and candles. Place the basket of stones on one side of the crucifix, and the basket containing the children's crosses on the other. If the Gospel story is not being dramatised, retell it to remind them of what happened. Then, with quiet music playing softly in the background, invite each child to take a stone and put it down next to the crucifix. Explain that they are putting down their stones just like the people in the crowd. This is a symbolic gesture of their regret and sorrow for past mistakes, and a sign of their willingness to be forgiving people. Then they pick up a cross which symbolises Christ's love and forgiveness for us, and which helps to remind us that we must be ready to love and forgive one another.

When everyone has returned to their place, conclude with a brief reading and closing prayer:

> Be loving, as your heavenly Father is loving.
> Do not judge,
> and you will not be judged yourselves;
> do not find fault in others,
> and they will not find fault in you;
> be forgiving, and you will be forgiven.
> However you treat others
> will be the way they treat you in return.
> (adapted from Luke 6:36-38)

Now our celebration together is drawing to a close, let us ask God our Father to forgive us as we forgive one another, as together we say the prayer which Jesus taught us:

Our Father,
who art in heaven . . .

• *Gospel dramatisation*

Using the narration script below as a guide, help
the children to dramatise the Gospel story through
mime and movement to music. Encourage them
to choose appropriate music to help set the
mood of the drama. You will need two people
to play the characters of Jesus and the woman,
and others to be the crowd which encircles her.
As the music begins, the woman moves quickly
around the chain of people holding hands which
is slowly circling around her. Wringing her hands
and wiping away imaginary tears, the woman
tries desperately to break through the circle and
escape, but her accusers push her back. The
circling crowd moves steadily faster, and, step-
ping forward, begins to close in around her.
Escape becomes impossible as she finds less space
in which to run and hide. The person playing
Jesus, meanwhile, has been sitting to one side,
calmly writing something on the ground next
to him.

As the music builds to a crescendo the woman
falls to her knees, covering her face with her
hands as the circle of people seems certain to
engulf her. Jesus gets to his feet and approaches
her accusers. Just as they raise their linked hands
ready to strike her, he raises his hands, and at
once the circle stops moving and everyone stands
perfectly still. Gently, he prises apart the arms of
two people to break the circle. As Jesus moves
towards the woman, the broken circle slowly
takes several paces back, and together they slowly
lower their upraised arms.

Jesus stands next to the woman who is kneel-
ing at his feet, head bowed in fear and hands
covering her face Stretching out his hand, he
points at the crowd and slowly turns to point at
each person in the circle. One by one, they release
each other's hands and bow their heads, before
taking several paces backwards, and then turning
and walking slowly away.

Jesus and the woman are left alone. Bending
down, he reaches out and helps her to her feet.
Slowly she opens her fingers and peers carefully
around her before taking her hands away from
her face. Jesus smiles at her and places one hand

reassuringly on her shoulder, and the other hand on his heart. The woman smiles at Jesus, and then places both of her hands on her own heart. Slowly she turns and walks away, turning to glance over her shoulder at the man who has given her a second chance.

(This drama could be performed after the Gospel, the reflection which follows, or as part of the liturgy of forgiveness.)

Narration script

The Pharisees brought a woman who had broken the Law to Jesus.
An angry crowd had gathered to stone her.
She stood within the circle of her accusers.
Imprisoned by her past mistakes. Without a future.
She stood in a circle without hope. She stood in a circle of fear.
Jesus did not defend the woman. He did not argue for a trial.
He simply broke the circle around her.
He changed the way people look at others.
He changed the way people look at themselves.
He freed her with forgiveness. He gave her a second chance.
So we ask ourselves . . .
Do we carry 'stones' which we need to put down?
Do we have someone or something we need to forgive?
Do we need to ask to be forgiven?

• The children could make the focal point for their celebration themselves, by arranging a collection of stones into the shape of a cross. These could simply be placed on the fabric background, or alternatively glued on to a suitably shaped template.

Music

- Suggestions are given below for dramatic and quiet music which could be used during the Gospel dramatisation.

  Dramatic
  Prokofiev: 'Dance of the Knights' from *Romeo and Juliet*
  Stravinsky: 'Dance of the Adolescents' from *The Rite of Spring*
  Orff: 'O Fortuna' from *Carmina Burana*

  Quiet
  Elgar: 'Nimrod' from *Enigma Variations*
  Rodrigo: Second movement (Adagio) from *Concierto de Aranjuez*

- O Lord, all the world belongs to you
  (LitHON/OS)

- Come back to me (LitHON)

- I'm accepted, I'm forgiven (OS)

8

Courage

Focus

On a large piece of blue cloth place a Bible opened at Matthew 14:25-33. Place a large dish, with some sand at the bottom and filled with water, in a suitable position on the display so that everyone has easy access to it. (A container used for floating candles is ideal.) Add additional props to the focus to create a stimulating and interesting seaside scene – for example, seashells, beach pebbles, glass nuggets, a model boat, pictures of the sea or waves, pieces of driftwood, sand. Small candles or nightlights can be dotted around the display. (Additional items can be added to this centrepiece depending on which particular ideas you choose to use for the liturgy.)

Introduction

We all need courage sometimes. There are times in our lives when we are called upon to be brave. Different things or situations can make us feel afraid or insecure, but, whatever they might be, we always feel better if we can face them with someone else beside us.

Penitential reflection

With suitable music playing quietly in the background, help the young people to spend time reflecting on the things or situations in their lives which make them feel uncomfortable with God and one another.

> Are there parts of my life which I would like to change?
> *(Pause)*
> things I regret and would do differently if I could go back and relive a particular moment;
> *(Pause)*
> things I have said or done about which I feel ashamed or sorry;
> *(Pause)*

parts of my life which come between me and
God's love;
    (Pause)
words I have spoken or things I have done to hurt
and upset my friends, my family, and those who
love me.
    (Pause)

God sees everything we hold in our hearts.
He knows us through and through.
There are no secrets from him.
He washes away our sins
just as waves wash away prints in the sand.

Now invite each person to come forward in turn,
and, using a finger, simply 'write' something they
would like God to forgive in the sand at the bottom
of the bowl of water before them, and watch their
words and sins symbolically 'disappear'.

Scripture   *Old Testament reading – adapted from Exodus 3:7-8, 10-12; 4:10-12*

Hearing the cries of the Israelite people who were
suffering cruelly at the hands of the Egyptians, God
called Moses before him and said, 'I have chosen
you to go to Pharaoh and lead my people out of
slavery in the land of Egypt.' But Moses asked God,
'How can someone as unimportant as me dare to
stand before the might of Pharaoh, or possibly
convince the Israelites to follow me?' 'There is
nothing to fear,' said God, 'because I will be with
you.' But Moses was still filled with self-doubt and
he said to God, 'Lord, as you have heard, I do not
speak quickly and struggle to get my words out.
Surely it would be wiser to send someone else!' But
God replied, 'Who has the power to give the gifts
of speech and hearing and sight? It is me, your
God. Now go, Moses! I shall tell you what to say
and make the words you use flow easily from
your mouth.'

Psalm – adapted from Psalm 17

Lord, you are the lamp which lights my way
and chases away the darkness.
Your hand protects and guides me
so I have nothing to fear.
You give me strength and courage,
you are the rock on which I can depend.

Gospel – adapted from Matthew 14:22-33

Jesus told his disciples to sail to the other side of the lake. Then he sent the crowds away and went up into the hills to pray alone. As night fell, the wind grew stronger and the disciples' boat was tossed about by the waves. In the darkness, just before dawn, Jesus came to them, walking on the sea, and they were terrified because they thought it was a ghost! But Jesus called to them, 'Don't be afraid, it's me!'

Peter shouted to Jesus, 'Lord, if that really is you, tell me to come to you across the water.' 'Come!' said Jesus. So Peter climbed out of the boat and lowered himself on to the water. Looking straight at Jesus, he began to walk towards him, but as he moved further from the boat and felt the strength of the wind, he grew afraid. Suddenly he began to sink and he cried out, 'Save me, Lord!' As Jesus reached out his hand and pulled Peter to safety, he said, 'Why did you not trust me, Peter? Is your belief so weak?' When they got back into the boat, the wind dropped and the other disciples knelt before Jesus and said, 'You are truly the Son of God.'

Reflection

Have you ever watched a young child take its very first steps? It is a very special moment which parents and families treasure for ever. As a baby grows stronger and more confident, it becomes bolder and more daring by trying out new manoeuvres which they have never attempted before. There is danger and risk in this process, and unless someone carefully watches over them, they can very quickly come to harm! But unless they take these risks, and step out into the unknown, they will never develop and learn the many different skills which they will need as adults. It is all part of nature's wonderful process of growing and maturing. Then, several years later, when the first rush of hormones plunges teenagers into the experience of adolescence, nature continues this careful process and encourages young people to take their next major brave and courageous steps into the adult world.

There are many different times in our lives when we feel the need for courage. Times when we step into the unknown, when our lives are filled with uncertainty and we may feel insecure and afraid. For young people it might be the challenge of facing exams, of beginning a new term, meeting new people, of changing school, or perhaps leaving home to find a job or to go to university.

But such challenges aren't confined to childhood and adolescence! They continue to test our courage and faith throughout our adult lives as well.

We have heard today how Moses and Peter both needed courage and faith in God to cope with the challenges they faced. Peter was asked to step from the safety and security of the boat and walk across the water towards Jesus. Would he sink beneath the waves, or could he really achieve the seemingly impossible feat of walking on water? For Peter there was only one way to find the answer to that question, and that required a huge step into the unknown – to leave the boat and have the courage to take that first uncertain step.

There will be many times in our lives when we will have to take just such a step, and choose whether or not we should do something. The decision will be ours, but it is important to remind ourselves that we will not be alone when we make it. Just as Moses and Peter had the reassuring presence of God to give them courage and faith, so God will always be beside us to encourage and support us through the many challenges we meet in our daily lives. Whenever we feel afraid, Jesus is always ready to reach out his hand, just as he did for Peter, to support and guide us through times of difficulty or doubt.

Intercession   As brothers and sisters in Christ,
let us ask our loving Father
to hear the prayers of his children:

For the courage to follow Christ
and bear witness to his Gospel
by sharing his love and forgiveness with the world.

Silence

Lord, hear us:
and answer our prayer.

For the courage to follow Christ
when it means standing up for what is right
and protecting the weak and defenceless.

Silence

Lord, hear us:
and answer our prayer.

For the courage to follow Christ
when we hear him calling us,
and to serve him in whatever way he asks of us.

Silence

Lord, hear us:
and answer our prayer.

For the courage to follow Christ
when others laugh at us
and poke fun because of what we believe.

Silence

Lord, hear us:
and answer our prayer.

For the courage to follow Christ
when we feel uncertain about which path to take
at difficult times of our lives.

Silence

Lord, hear us:
and answer our prayer.

Knowing that our heavenly Father is listening,
in the silence of our hearts
let us share our own unspoken prayers with him.

Silence

God of patient love,
hear our prayers,
and give us the courage to follow
when we hear you call.
If we lose our way,
guide us back to the path
which leads to your heavenly kingdom.
We ask this in the name of Christ our Lord.
Amen.

Activities and ideas

• *Meditation*

The children can be sitting on chairs, lying on the floor, or with their heads down and arms crossed on their desks, depending on what is most practical. Ask them to remove their shoes and place their feet flat on the floor. Give them time to settle themselves before you begin.

Read the text very slowly in a calm voice. Pause at full stops for at least five seconds. Read the relaxation steps even more slowly, and as you move towards the meditation, allow the pauses to become longer. Pace yourself carefully and allow a sufficient period of at least five minutes silence at the end before leading them out of the meditation.

Have a recording of sea sounds playing softly in the background to add to the atmosphere, or use appropriate music of your own choice.

Close your eyes. Take a deep breath and relax. Check that you are comfortable, whether you are sitting or lying down.

Listen to the sounds around you – identify them and then let them drift away into the background.

Feel the breath entering and leaving your body. Cool air breathed in, warm air breathed out.

Don't hold the breath, find your own natural rhythm, in and out, in and out.

Screw up the muscles of your face into a frown and hold them tight. Now relax – feel the tension drain away.

Hunch your shoulders up towards your ears and hold the tension. Now relax – feel the tension drain away.

Clench your hands into tight fists. Feel the muscles in your arm go taut. Hold the clench – and then relax. Let the tension drain away.

Check your breathing – cool air in, warm air out.

Curl your toes up as tightly as you can. Feel the muscles in your leg go taut. Hold that tension – now let it go.

Make sure that you are still comfortable – slowly adjust your position if you need to.

It is early in the morning and the sun is coming up. You are in a boat on the Sea of Galilee. Hear the waves lapping gently against its sides. See the red sky. Feel the gentle warmth of the early morning sun on your face.
Lick your lips as they are moistened by the gentle sea breeze.

You have watched Jesus walking across the water towards the boat.
He is smiling. 'Do not be afraid,' you hear him say.
Now you watch as he stretches out his hand and beckons.
He is looking at Peter. Peter is uncertain what to do.
He is sitting astride the boat. He is on the edge.
One foot is almost touching the water below.
One foot is firmly in the boat.
He hesitates. You share his fear and doubt.
Then suddenly he is gone. He steps from the boat and you see him smile.

The doubt returns and he hesitates.
Surely the water will swallow him.
But Jesus reaches out and he is safe.

Now it is your turn to take a big step in your life.
A step into new water, the unknown.
It will need all your courage, and you feel uncertain and afraid.
You see that Jesus is still standing there. He is not far away.
He smiles and beckons.
He reaches out his hand towards you.
You are not alone. He will keep you safe.
Are you ready to take that step?

Slowly become aware of your own body. Feel the seat or floor beneath you.

Slowly and gently move your fingers and toes.

Listen to your breath. Cool breath in, warm breath out.

When you feel ready, come back into the room and slowly open your eyes.

• *Footprint pictures*

You will need some poster paint, brushes, coloured paper to print on, an old tray or large plate, and some bowls of water and old towels.
Arrange the children's chairs in a circle. If numbers are large they will have to take turns to make their pictures. Give each child a large square of coloured paper and ask them to place it on the floor in front of the chair where they are sitting. When they have removed their shoes and socks, apply a fairly thick layer of paint to the soles of both feet. Then ask them to stand on the coloured paper in front of them carefully so that they don't smudge the prints. They can then step off the paper into a bowl of water to wash their feet. Make the posters colourful and interesting by using different colours of paint and background paper.

• *Footprint prayer cards*

Photocopy the adaptations of Psalms 22 and 61 below. Help the children to stick one of these on to some rectangles of card. Pour some poster paint into a shallow container and show the children how to make a 'footprint' image by clenching their hand and then dipping the edge (little-finger side) of their hand into the paint before carefully pressing it on to the back of the prayer card. (A left hand will produce a left 'footprint' and the right hand a right 'footprint.') By dipping their thumb and index finger into the paint, they can then add 'toe-print' shapes to complete the image of the footprint they have created.

Trust in God
The Good Shepherd takes care of all my needs.
He leads me to lush green meadows
where I can rest,
and crystal clear pools to refresh me.
He protects me from every kind of danger
and guides me along the path of goodness.
When night falls, and darkness surrounds me,
I am not afraid.
I know that God is always beside me
to calm all my fears.
Adapted from Psalm 22:1-4

Trust in God
In God alone can I find rest.
He keeps me safe from harm,
he is the rock which stands firm
when the world around me
quivers with uncertainty.
I can always depend on him
to offer shelter in times of trouble
when he hears my heartfelt cries.
Adapted from Psalm 61:5-8

• *Liturgy of courage*

Prepare an altar or prayer table with a candle to symbolise Christ surrounded by some seashells and pebbles, and a dish filled with water and some floating candles. Place a wicker basket on the table. On small pieces of paper the children write one thing for which they feel they need courage, or draw a picture or symbol of one of their fears. They then fold their pieces of paper. Invite them to place these in the basket next to the Christ light. Choose one child to light the floating candles using a taper, as you remind the children that Jesus is always close by to give us courage and keep us afloat at times when we really need him to reach out and help us. Finish by listening to or singing a suitable hymn or song together.

Music

- 'I'll be at your side' by The Corrs
- 'Bridge over troubled waters' by Simon and Garfunkel
- Do not be afraid (LitHON/OS)
- Christ be beside me (LitHON/OS)
- Father, I place into your hands (LitHON/OS)
- Walk with me, O my Lord (LitHON/OS)
- I, the Lord of sea and sky (LitHON/OS)
- Will you come and follow me (LitHON)
- Yahweh, I know you are near (LitHON/OS)
- Put your trust (LitHON/OS)

9

Gifts from God

Focus   Prepare a floor or table display using a background cloth, a Bible open at Matthew 25:14-27, a candle or candles, and either a crucifix or a picture or icon of Christ. (Additional elements of the focus will be determined by whichever activity idea you choose to use for this celebration.)

Introduction   When we love someone, one way to express the love we feel for them is with a gift. As an expression of God's immense love for each one of us, he gives us special gifts which are unique to every individual.

Penitential reflection   When we use our talents and gifts unwisely
or waste them:
Father, forgive us.
Father, forgive us.

When we use our talents and gifts selfishly
and abuse them:
Jesus, forgive us.
Jesus, forgive us.

When we deny our talents and gifts
and hide them away:
Father, forgive us.
Father, forgive us.

Scripture   *New Testament reading – adapted from Acts 2:1-11*

The disciples had gathered together in Jerusalem to celebrate the Feast of Pentecost and to wait for the Holy Spirit whom Jesus had promised to send.

One day, as they were praying together, the room was suddenly filled with the sound of a powerful wind which roared through the house. Then, what looked like small tongues of fire appeared and spread out to touch each one of them. So it was that they were filled with the Holy Spirit.

At once, in their excitement, they rushed outside to tell everyone what had happened to them. As they began to speak, they were amazed to find that everyone listening to their words could understand them! People from different regions and countries were astounded to hear these men preaching to them in their own native languages.

New Testament reading – adapted from 1 Corinthians 12:4-11

There are many different gifts, but each gift is given by the same Spirit; there are many different ways to serve, but all service is to the same God. Whatever manner of work we do, it is the same God who works in each of us. The Spirit acts in and through each person for the benefit of all. He gives a variety of different gifts to different individuals; to some he gives wisdom; to some knowledge; and to others he gives the gift of faith. Whatever gift is generously given is to be used lovingly for the good of one another.

Gospel – adapted from Matthew 25:14-27

Jesus told the people a parable: 'The master of a household was going abroad for some time, so he called for his servants and said to them, "I am splitting my property between you according to your skill for managing it." He gave each man a number of talents which were equivalent to several years' wages. To the first he gave five talents, to the second he gave two, and the third man received one. The first two men used their talents wisely, and soon doubled the amount they had been given. The man who received only one talent hid it away out of sight.

'A long time later, the master of the house returned from his travels and called for his servants to see how they had invested his money. The first two servants stepped forward and presented him with double the amount they had been given. "Well done," the master said. "Now I know that you can be trusted with small amounts, I shall certainly trust you with more. Come and celebrate with me!" Then the third servant stepped forward and returned to his master exactly what he had been given. His master was furious and said to him, "You useless, lazy man! Even if you had simply put this amount in the bank, with interest it would have made more!"'

Reflection   We have all been blessed with talents from God. Some are obvious for all to see, some take time to develop and grow, and some remain hidden away until they suddenly appear and surprise us at particular moments of our lives. Every individual has been given different gifts measured out in different amounts by God. We are reminded in today's Gospel parable that we each have a responsibility to make the best use of the talents God has given to us. Instead of hiding them away and being afraid to reveal them, we should use them well and encourage them to grow. Just like the servants in the story Jesus told, we will each be called to account by our Master when he returns; he will want to know what we have done with the precious talents he has entrusted to us.

God knows and understands that at times this can be something which we find rather daunting and challenging, and that all too often we are tempted to act like the servant who simply wanted a quiet life without hassle, who buried the talent and left it untouched and unused. So God sends the Holy Spirit to help us by bringing his own very special gifts to share with us. The seven gifts of the Spirit which we receive when we are confirmed – wisdom, understanding, right judgement, reverence, courage, knowledge, and awe and wonder – enable and help us to use all our talents to their fullest potential, for the glory of God and the benefit of one another.

At different times in our lives and in different situations, we will find that we particularly need to call upon a special gift of the Holy Spirit. It might be the gift of courage when we want the strength to do what is right in a difficult situation; it might be the gift of understanding to help us make sense of what God asks us to do and of the world around us; it might be the gifts of wisdom and knowledge to allow us to 'see' the world as Christ does, and make choices which help us to follow his Gospel of love and forgiveness.

So today let us make time in our lives to take a good look at ourselves, to recognise and give thanks for all the marvellous gifts we have been given, and to reflect upon how well we use them in our daily lives.

Intercession

As we gather before God our Father,
we ask him to hear and answer
the needs of all his people:

Let us pray for peace in our troubled world;
may we use the gift of our talents
to promote peace in our homes, our schools
and our everyday lives.

Silence

Loving Lord:
let us do your will.

Let us pray for the homeless and hungry;
may we use the gift of our talents
to relieve their suffering and hardship.

Silence

Loving Lord:
let us do your will.

Let us pray for people who feel hopeless and alone;
may we use the gift of our talents
to help them to feel valued,
and to realise that every individual
has something good to share with the world.

Silence

Loving Lord:
let us do your will.

Let us pray for one another;
may we use the gifts of the Holy Spirit
to help and guide us to become more like Christ,
who showed us how to love and forgive one another.

Silence

Loving Lord:
let us do your will.

Knowing that our heavenly Father is listening,
in the silence of our hearts
let us share our own unspoken prayers with him.

Silence

God of goodness,
may we use the gifts you have given wisely,
so that they may bring us closer
to your loving kingdom.
We ask this through Christ our Lord.
Amen.

Activities and ideas

• (This exercise, which is intended to help children to discover their own potential and to look for and recognise the many gifts they have to offer amongst themselves, assumes that the group members know each other reasonably well.)

Sit in groups of 8-10 in a circle, each person with a piece of paper and something to write with. Ask them to listen carefully to the words of the reading from Corinthians.

Now invite them (in silence or with music playing quietly in the background) to write their name at the top of their sheet of paper, and to spend a few moments thinking of two or three gifts they have. Ask them to write these down and then pass their sheet on to the next person sitting on their right. They should look at the name at the top of the sheet, and add a gift which they feel that person has to the list. This continues around the circle until each person's sheet is returned to them.

Now invite the children to spend a few moments reading and thinking about their gifts and what others have written about them. Encourage the children to discuss and share the many gifts they have between them, and any practical ways they can think of for using them well. Close with a short prayer thanking God for one another and the gifts you have discovered during this activity.

- You will need to add to the focus the seven gifts of the Holy Spirit (wisdom, understanding, right judgement, courage, knowledge, awe and wonder, reverence) printed or written on slips of coloured paper for the children to select and collect from the display. (You will need several copies of each gift.) You will also need a gift-wrapped box or container.

  With reflective music playing in the background, hand out slips of paper and pencils, and invite each child to reflect about, and then write down, a gift which they have been given. Ask them to consider which, if any, of the seven gifts of the Spirit they would most appreciate at this moment of their lives.

  Invite them to come forward and place their 'gifts' anonymously in a gift-wrapped box or container on the focus/display as an offering to God, and to collect a copy of any gifts of the Spirit which they feel they need or would like. Allow a few moments of quiet reflection before closing with a prayer of thanksgiving or by singing a hymn together.

- You will need enough flowers cut from paper to allow for one for each child, and a large bowl (or several small ones) with coloured pebbles or glass beads at the bottom to add interest. (The types of bowls used for floating candles are ideal.)

Give each child a paper flower and a colour-fast pen or pencil. Ask them to write a gift they have, or a letter or symbol to represent that gift, in the central part of the flower. When they have done this, fold the petals towards the centre to cover what they have written or drawn. Invite each child to place their flower carefully on the water with its folded petals uppermost. As they watch, the petals will slowly unfold before their eyes, symbolising how our God-given gifts will blossom and come alive in our lives.

Music

- All that I am (LitHON/OS)
- Taizé music, particularly 'Veni Sancti Spiritus' (LitHON)
- Gifts of bread and wine (LitHON/OS)
- Lord, accept the gifts we offer (LitHON)
- In the love of God and neighbour (LitHON/OS)
- Holy Spirit of fire (LitHON/OS)
- O my Lord, within my heart (LitHON/OS)

10

—— Don't be sad – a celebration of life ——

Focus

A table or floor display with a Bible open at John 14:1-3; a (paschal) candle; a crucifix or cross.

Introduction

Jesus knew how it felt to be sad. He experienced the pain and grief we feel when someone we know and love dies. At such times in our lives, Jesus understands and shares those moments of pain in a very special and personal way.

Penitential reflection

When we turn from God and choose another path which leads us away from his love:
Father, forgive us.
Father, forgive us.

When our words and actions make us unworthy to be called children of God:
Jesus, forgive us.
Jesus, forgive us.

When we forget that we must be ready to forgive, as we are forgiven:
Father, forgive us.
Father, forgive us.

Scripture

New Testament reading – adapted from 1 Thessalonians 4:13, 14, 17, 18

Do not weep for those who have died, or be filled with sadness like those who have nothing to hope for. We believe that Jesus died and rose to new life, and that the same thing will happen to all who believe in him. Take comfort in knowing that everyone who dies in Christ shall rise to new life and be with him for ever.

Gospel – adapted from John 14:1-3

Jesus said, 'Do not feel sad and downhearted. Just as you trust in my Father, so you can trust in me. My Father's house has many rooms, and I will make one ready for you. When a place has been prepared, I will come back for you, and we will be together. You already know the way to the place where I am going.'

Gospel – adapted from John 11:1-45

Lazarus and his two sisters, Martha and Mary, were very good friends of Jesus. They lived in a town called Bethany, not far from Jerusalem. One day, the sisters sent an urgent message to Jesus, because Lazarus was very ill and close to death. Hearing this message, Jesus said, 'This illness will not bring death for Lazarus, but glory for God and his Son,' and he did not set off immediately, even though he was very fond of Lazarus and his sisters. When Jesus and his disciples arrived in Bethany more than two days later, they found that Lazarus was dead and had already been buried for four days. Martha ran to meet Jesus and said to him, 'Lord, if you had been here, you could have saved our brother.' Jesus said, 'Your brother will live again.' 'I know that on the last day he will come back to life,' she answered. Jesus turned to her and said, 'I am the resurrection and the life. Anyone who believes in me will have eternal life, and he will never die. Do you believe this?' Martha answered him, 'Yes, Lord, because I know that you are the Christ, the Son of God.'

When Jesus saw the great sadness of Martha and Mary and their friends, he wept with love and sorrow. 'Show me where he is buried,' he said. So they took him to the tomb, where Jesus said to them, 'Roll away the stone, and you will see God's glory.'

'Lord,' Martha said, 'Lazarus has been dead for four days and by now he will smell.' Jesus said to her, 'You will see God's glory if you believe in me.' So they did as he said, and, looking up to heaven, Jesus prayed, 'Father, I thank you, for I know that you always listen to me. Let these people see and believe.' Then he called out in a loud voice, 'Lazarus, come out!' To everyone's amazement

Lazarus appeared, still wrapped in burial cloths, and walked from the tomb. Many people saw what happened that day, and they believed in Jesus.

Reflection

Have you ever admired an intricate and detailed piece of needlework or tapestry, and marvelled at the thousands of threads and stitches which together create the picture. If we stand too close to such a piece of work, it can be hard to make out what it is; we need to stand back to appreciate and understand the image before us. If you ever turn such a marvellous creation over and look at the back of the piece of work, you would be equally amazed to see a jumble of intricate knots and loose threads. The whole thing looks a complete mess, and it is almost impossible to guess what the picture on the other side might be.

Life can be compared to such a tapestry, with God the master weaver who is the only one who knows what the final picture will look like. As he busily weaves and helps us to direct the threads of our lives, it is as though we are standing at the back of the tapestry, where we are unable to make out the final picture. We must trust him to direct our efforts, even at times when things seem to be going badly in our lives.

When someone we know or love dies, we can find it difficult to understand why such a sad thing has happened. We are unable to 'see' where it fits into God's plan for the tapestry of life. For a time it can seem that our sadness and grief will stop us from working our part of that tapestry ever again. It is difficult to understand how life goes on as normal, as people around us go about their everyday business, and seem unaware of our heartache and sorrow. Our lives and the lives of those around us can take twists and turns like threads, and we can see no pattern nor make any sense of the direction they sometimes take. We cannot see the final picture which God is in the process of creating.

When someone dies, Jesus understands our feelings of grief, and shares our sadness and loss in a very special way. But, as the readings we have listened to tell us, he gives us hope and the joyful promise of everlasting life with him. Although it is right that we express our sadness when someone dies, it is also good to celebrate their life and to rejoice at their happiness of finding peace with God in the place he has prepared especially for them in heaven.

There they are able to stand on the other side of the tapestry, and see the final picture of God's glory. They will finally be able to understand how the twists and turns in their lives were all part of God's elaborate plan, as the threads of their life become part of his wonderful tapestry.

Intercession

With love in our hearts,
let us unite as one family
to ask God for all our needs:

Christ was driven away
by those who did not listen or understand;
may people who are driven from their homes,
their families, and their land,
find forgiveness in their hearts
and comfort in their sorrow.

Silence

We pray to the Lord:
Lord, hear us.

Christ was betrayed and let down by his friends;
may we be forgiven for the times
when we betray his friendship
and turn our backs on his love
and the love of others.

Silence

We pray to the Lord:
Lord, hear us.

Christ was imprisoned and tortured
for the sake of goodness;
may all who suffer such cruelty and imprisonment
for just causes

be strengthened by their closeness to God
and our cries for their freedom.

Silence

We pray to the Lord:
Lord, hear us.

Christ wept at the death of his friend Lazarus;
may the tears of sadness
of those who mourn for a loved one
become tears of joy
with the promise of their resurrection and eternal
life.

Silence

We pray to the Lord:
Lord, hear us.

Christ was laid in the darkness of the tomb;
may those whose lives are overshadowed
by sadness and grief
be enlightened by the knowledge
that Christ shares their sorrow,
and may they draw comfort from his presence.

Silence

We pray to the Lord:
Lord, hear us.

Knowing that our heavenly Father is listening,
in the silence of our hearts
let us share our own unspoken prayers with him.

Silence

Lord God,
we ask you to receive our prayers
and answer them
according to your holy will.
We make these prayers through Christ our Lord.
Amen.

Activities and ideas

- The cross is the most important symbol of the Christian faith. We can look beyond it and see the risen Christ, and be reminded that suffering and death will end in resurrection and new life. Help the children to make bookmarks decorated with a cross. You will need pieces of hessian material or aida fabric cut into bookmark shapes; pieces of squared paper for marking out their designs; darning needles and coloured yarn or fine wool.

- Encourage the children to create a wax and paint picture of someone or some event they especially want to remember. Arrange the children in pairs or small evenly sized groups, and encourage them to spend some time quietly reflecting about the subject of their picture. Then give each child a sheet of white paper and a piece of white candle with which to draw an invisible image. They will need to press down firmly as they draw. When they have written their own name at the top of the paper, ask each child to exchange their paper with another child. They paint carefully over the top of the picture with thin paint. As the paint fails to cover the wax, the picture will emerge. In their pairs or small groups they can share and explain what they have drawn. Their pictures can be used as a display or as part of the central focus.

- Enlarge a suitable line drawing of an image or scene. Using a light pencil, divide the picture into a series of equally sized squares which are numbered in order on the back. (There should be sufficient squares to allow at least one per child.) Cut out the numbered squares. On another piece of paper, draw a grid of corresponding numbered squares and pin or stick this to a suitable surface. Have an assortment of different coloured felt-tip pens for the children to choose from. With reflective music playing quietly in the background, ask each child to come forward and collect a square of paper and some pens. They should then return to their places, and carefully and in silence, colour the side which has no number written on it. They should use as many colours as they like to completely cover all the white paper. When they have completed this task, ask them to check the number of their piece of paper, and then use a small piece of blue-tack to stick their individual square on the correspondingly numbered square on the grid. As each child adds a square, a mosaic effect picture of the final image should gradually appear. Using 'Blu-Tack' allows you to rearrange the pictures neatly to create a final image which can clearly be made out. Just as in a tapestry, each person's contribution contributes a vital part in creating the final and complete picture.

- Have some dead leaves scattered around the display. After listening to one of the readings, allow a quiet time for reflection, before inviting the children to collect a leaf in memory of some-one who has died. They touch the open Bible with it, before placing it at the base of the candle, which is surrounded by fresh flowers or buds to represent new life.

- Place a tray of soil or compost on the focal display together with a container of seeds which can be easily picked up – nasturtiums or sunflowers, for example. Read the extract from Matthew's Gospel below, and then invite the children to take a seed and push it into the tray of soil, as a symbolic gesture of new life. The tray can later be posi-tioned so that the children can see the seeds growing.

  How does a seed grow? Night and day, while we are asleep and while we are awake, it sprouts and grows; and no one quite knows how. Until finally the crop is ready and the harvest can be gathered in. (Adapted from Matthew 4:27-29)

Music
- Be still and know I am with you (LitHON/OS)
- I am the Bread of Life (LitHON/OS)
- Walk with me, O my Lord (LitHON/OS)
- Lord of all hopefulness (LitHON/OS)
- Vivaldi: 'Spring' from *The Four Seasons*
- Rodrigo: Second movement (Adagio) from *Concierto de Aranjuez*

11

Friendship

Focus   A Bible open at Luke 10:30-37, a large candle, and a picture or icon of Jesus. Additional props should be added to the focus to reflect the choice of readings you make and the activity idea(s) you use.

Introduction   Listen together to 'Eleanor Rigby' by The Beatles, or 'Solitaire' sung by The Carpenters, encouraging the children to think about several questions as they do so:

- What does this song say about loneliness?

- Why are some people lonely?

- How does it make people feel to have no friends?

Everyone needs friends, and we all know that true and lasting friendship takes time to blossom and grow. Friendship means making time for one another, sharing our hopes and dreams, and seeing each other through both good times and bad. Jesus is our perfect friend. His friendship enriches and changes the lives of everyone who is touched by his love and forgiveness.

Penitential reflection   Let us ask for God's forgiveness
for the times we spoil our friendship
with him or one another.

Jesus, friend of sinners:
Lord, have mercy.
Lord, have mercy.

Jesus, our forgiving friend:
Christ, have mercy.
Christ, have mercy.

Jesus who befriends the friendless:
Lord, have mercy.
Lord, have mercy.

Scripture   *New Testament reading – adapted from Romans 14:10-13, 19; 15:2*

Do not judge one another, because we have only one judge and that is God. Instead encourage one another to lead good lives which will please God. Always look for ways in which you can help others and share the peace of Christ with them. Put your neighbour's needs before your own, just as Jesus did, and let your thoughtfulness for each other unite you in love.

Gospel

(A selection is provided from which an appropriate reading can be chosen for a specific occasion.)

Jesus calls us to be his friends – adapted from Mark 1:16-20

One day while he was walking beside the Sea of Galilee, Jesus saw Simon and his brother Andrew casting their nets to catch fish. He called out to them, 'Come, follow me and I will make you fishers of people.' The brothers left their nets and followed him. Further along the shore Jesus saw James and his brother John who were mending nets with their father Zebedee. Jesus called them too, and at once they left their father and followed him.

Jesus is friend of the lonely – adapted from Luke 19:1-10

Jesus went to a town called Jericho, where a man called Zacchaeus lived. He was a chief tax collector who was very rich. When Jesus arrived, crowds gathered to see him, and Zacchaeus was among them. Zacchaeus was very small and could not see Jesus because of the crowds, so he went on ahead and climbed a tree to get a better view. As Jesus passed by, he looked up and said, 'Come, Zacchaeus. Hurry down! I want to visit your house today.' Zacchaeus climbed down quickly and made Jesus welcome. Seeing all this, the crowd began to grumble and complain. 'How can Jesus agree to be the guest of such a wicked man?' they said.

Then Zacchaeus turned to Jesus and said, 'Lord, I will give half of everything I own to the poor, and pay back everything I have stolen four times over.' Jesus smiled at Zacchaeus and said, 'Today this house knows salvation! You, too, Zacchaeus, are a son of Abraham. The Son of Man came to save anyone who has lost their way.'

Jesus is friend of the sick – adapted from Mark 1:29-31

Jesus left the synagogue and went to the house where Simon Peter and his brother Andrew lived. When they arrived at the house Jesus was told that Simon Peter's mother-in-law had been taken ill and was suffering from a fever. Jesus went to her, took her by the hand and, as he helped her up, the fever disappeared and she felt well again.

Jesus is friend of sinners – adapted from Luke 7:36-48

One of the Pharisees called Simon invited Jesus to dinner. A woman who had done many things she was ashamed of heard that Jesus would be there and came to find him. She knelt at his feet and began to cry, wiping her tears from his feet with her long hair, before covering them with kisses and perfumed ointment.

Simon was annoyed that Jesus would allow such a sinful person near him. But Jesus knew what Simon was thinking and asked him, 'If one servant owed his master fifty pounds and another owed his master five thousand pounds, which one would love his master more if the debts were cancelled?' 'The one who owed more,' Simon answered.

Then Jesus said, 'Simon, you did not offer me water to wash my feet with, a kiss as a greeting, or perfume to refresh me. This woman has done all these things and more. Surely her many sins have been forgiven, for her to show such great love. Where little has been forgiven, little love is shown.' And he said to the woman, 'Your sins are indeed forgiven.'

Jesus is friend to all – adapted from Luke 10:30-37

A teacher of the Law once asked Jesus, 'Who is my neighbour?'

In reply Jesus told him this story: 'One day a man was travelling from Jerusalem to Jericho, when a gang of robbers attacked him. They beat him up, and after stealing everything he had, they left him lying half dead by the roadside. A short time later, one of the Temple priests passed that way, but he crossed the road and walked on by. Soon, another traveller came, but he too passed by on the other side of the road. Then a Samaritan came along, and when he saw the injured man he took pity on him. He bandaged his wounds, and carried him on horseback to a nearby inn. There he cared for him and when the time came for him to leave, he left the innkeeper enough money to pay for the man's room until he was better.'

Jesus then asked the teacher, 'Which man in the story was a good neighbour?' 'The one who helped the wounded traveller,' he answered. 'Go then and do the same,' said Jesus.

Reflection

Have you ever thrown a rock or pebble into a pool of still water and watched what happens next? That one small pebble sets in motion a whole series of ripples which travel outwards in waves from the point at which the pebble hits the water, until they finally stop when they meet something in their path. The single action of throwing that small stone has far-reaching effects which carry on even after the pebble has disappeared from sight and is forgotten.

Our lives are rather like that pool, and every so often someone throws a pebble of friendship, which sends out far-reaching ripples of love. One small act of friendship can affect the lives and happiness of many people around us. Take, for example, the story of Jesus and Zacchaeus!

Zacchaeus was a wealthy tax collector who gained his fortune by cheating his fellow Jews, and as a result no one liked him. When Jesus met Zacchaeus and went to share a meal at his house, that one small gesture of friendship (just like the pebble in the pool) changed the life of Zacchaeus for ever. He valued the friendship of Jesus so much that he decided to turn over a new leaf and become a kinder and more honest person. The 'ripples' from this friendly act also affected the other tax collectors Zacchaeus knew, as he in turn invited them in friendship to meet this man who had shown him a new and better way of life. But the ripples didn't stop there. The people who had seen what Jesus had done were at first horrified to think that he could even consider befriending such a disagreeable and dishonest character. The ripples of his action hit them when they realised that Jesus offered his friendship to everyone, because everyone was his neighbour and deserved his love, and he expected them to do the same. We hear no more about what happened to Zacchaeus, but chances are he discovered what it meant to receive and share friendship in a way he had never done before.

Jesus welcomed tax collectors, lepers, people with physical or mental illnesses, and anyone who was alone and friendless. He made sure that his actions spoke louder than words, and showed the world the meaning of true friendship by sharing his time, his love and his forgiveness with them. He challenges us to do the same in whatever way we can in our everyday lives.

It is easy for us to be friends with people we like and enjoy spending time with. Even on that odd occasion when we might fall out and have a disagreement about something, true friendship means that it is never very long before we say sorry and make up. It is much harder to offer our friendship to people we do not like, but Jesus expects us to treat and love everyone equally. He understands that we can find this difficult, but he still wants us to try. Jesus calls each one of us to be his friend, and to follow his loving example and share his life. He took every available opportunity to befriend those who would otherwise have been without a friend in the world.

The readings we have listened to today tell us quite clearly that there are many different ways to be a friend to someone. It might mean being ready to forgive a person for something they have or have not done; it might mean spending time with someone who is lonely, or caring for someone who is feeling a bit under the weather; it might be as simple as a warm smile or a welcoming hello. Being a friend to someone doesn't need dramatic and grand gestures; it simply means being there for them and thinking about their needs and happiness. Just like the small pebble and the many ripples it produces, a simple smile can spread out to touch and brighten the lives of many people around us.

So what will your pebble of friendship be today?

Intercession   God our loving Father,
with simple trust and humble hope
we your children come before you
with all our needs:

We pray for friendship in the Church
and among all her people;
as we devote our lives
to bringing the values of God's kingdom
into the world,
may we share the gift of friendship
with our neighbours
of every race, colour and religion.

Silence

Father of friendship:
fill our lives with love.

We pray for friendship in our homes and families;
as we grow together in love and respect,
may we also grow in understanding
about what it means to share the friendship of Christ,
by judging no one
and touching lives with love and understanding.

Silence

Father of friendship:
fill our lives with love.

We pray for greater friendship
to be shown towards the poor, the homeless
and those who are outcasts;
as we follow in the footsteps of Christ,
may our actions and words show
the compassionate friendship of Christ,
who saw no one as being beyond the reach
of God's grace
or his message of love and forgiveness.

Silence

Father of friendship:
fill our lives with love.

We pray for friendship
between the nations and religions of the world;
as children of God, may we respect and accept
our neighbours far and near,
forgiving past mistakes
and striving to fill our world
with peace and understanding.

Silence

Father of friendship:
fill our lives with love.

Knowing that our heavenly Father is listening,
in the silence of our hearts
let us share our own unspoken prayers with him.

Silence

Father, may your loving friendship
guide our daily lives.
By knowing and loving you
may we know and love our neighbour,
and become a friend to everyone we meet.
We ask this through Christ our Lord.
Amen.

Activities and ideas

- Using three or four lengths of brightly coloured wool or yarn, help the children to plait 'friendship bracelets' which they can give to one another.

- Place a shallow container filled with water and a layer of sand on the central display, together with a collection of small pebbles or coloured glass beads sitting next to it. With quiet music playing in the background, invite the children to reflect silently on ways in which they can share the gift of friendship with others – at school, at home, with people they meet every day in the community in which they live. As a symbol of their chosen act of friendship, ask them to come forward one by one and gently drop a pebble into the dish of water and watch the ripples it makes.

- Give the children sheets of coloured paper and ask them to trace carefully around their hands. Cut out the hand shapes they have made, and arrange them around a large paper picture of the world to create a colourful banner or display.

- You will need shapes of human figures (boys and girls) cut out of thin card or thick paper.

  Ask the children to think about and then name the qualities they look for in a friend. Write these on a large sheet of paper which everyone can see. Then invite them to choose a figure to represent their best friend. On one side they should write, or copy from the list you have made, the quality of friendship they most value, and on the other colour in their figure. These can be displayed on a board, a mobile, a banner or picture, or stapled together in different sized circles which stand freely.

- With suitable dressing-up props, encourage the children to dramatise one or more of the Gospel examples of Jesus befriending different people. Ask them to make up their own modern-day equivalent of the story.

- Give the children a selection of newspapers and magazines, and encourage them to find articles and stories about examples of friendship. These can be cut out, read and discussed, and their favourites mounted on a display. The children could then write an illustrated story or poem about an act of friendship in their own lives, either made by them or by someone they know. These should be displayed alongside the magazine and newspaper articles.

Music
- Zacchaeus was a very little man (LitHON/OS)
- Jesus had all kinds of friends (LitHON/OS)